"My friend Stan Endicott loves the church and always brings a kingdom perspective. Highly relational, he builds into others in all he does. In this new book, *Reflect,* Stan brings together 52 stories from worship leaders from across the United States. Most are worship leaders Stan has personally mentored or coached".

—Warren Bird
Director of Research and Intellectual Capital
Leadership Network

"I could not begin to count how many worship leaders and church artists have sat across a table with a cup of tea or coffee with Stan Endicott, as I have many times. Stan is the most loving and effective mentor I know. He listens attentively, asks tremendous questions, and then grabs a paper napkin and draws something brilliant that leads to a personal breakthrough. I celebrate how God designed Stan and consider him to be a stealth weapon for growth in the kingdom! I know *Reflect* will be a terrific tool for artists and worshipers everywhere"

—Nancy Beach
Champion for the Arts
Willow Creek Association

"To find one source where 52 of some of our nation's best worship leaders reflect on life and ministry is like a pot of gold. . . . a wealth of knowledge and wisdom as a result of ministry done well. Hats off to Stan Endicott who I have witnessed (from a front row seat) become the master of relational connectivity! As a mentor, friend, and partner in life and work, Stan brings out the best in me and all who have the privilege of knowing him."

—Monty Kelso
Worship Pastor
Slingshot Group Partner

REFLECT
FIFTY-TWO STORIES FOR WORSHIPERS

COMPILED BY **STAN ENDICOTT**

BEACON HILL PRESS
OF KANSAS CITY

Library of Congress Cataloging-in-Publication Data

Endicott, Stan.
   Reflect : fifty-two stories for worshipers / by Stan Endicott.
      p. cm.
   ISBN 978-0-8341-2605-3 (hardcover)
  1. Christian life—Meditations. I. Title.
   BV4501.3.E53 2011
   248.4—dc22

                                                            2011013155

10 9 8 7 6 5 4 3 2 1

CONTENTS

INTRODUCTION
MY HEART TO YOURS

My life is centered by wonderful people whom I love and who love me. Growing up in a small church in the small town of Woodlawn, Illinois, I got to know people well. When there are only 350 people in the entire town, you know them all, you see them often, you spend time with them, and you become a wonderful community—in this case a fun little village. The railroad tracks ran right through the middle of town, with about twenty houses on each side. We also had a grade school—where I was a star basketball player—a high school, a post office, a small grocery store, my dad's furniture store, and a café with two pool tables, two pinball machines, and the best cheeseburgers and banana cream pie in the entire world. How could life be more fun for a kid than that?

This small-town, Midwest culture taught me so much about life, but probably the main lesson I learned was how important relationships are to our personal lives. I had about forty friends my age, as well as friends younger and older than me. In fact, some of the people who invested in my life were fifty, sixty, even seventy years older than me. Thank you, Woodlawn! You "marked" me in wonderful ways. You taught me to love people and have a curious spirit.

This book brings me great joy because of my relationship with the contributors. I know the people who have written these great life lessons. Some I don't know well, but many I have coached or mentored. There are also a few who are close friends. I love them all. I love what they are doing for the people in their own lives. I love what they are doing for Christ and the local church. When we hear stories of others, we are encouraged, moved, changed.

My dad, a World War II fighter pilot, taught me so many things about life. In fact both my mom and dad taught me to love life, to look for new, fun, "adventuresome" experiences. I am grateful to them for that. But Dad, a Hellcat pilot on an aircraft carrier in the Pacific, told me, "Son, headwind will either crash your plane or give you lift. Always make sure your wings are pointed in the right direction to give you lift. You will face headwind often, but use it to your advantage."

My relationship with Jesus started when I was twelve. That summer, during Vacation Bible School, I put on Christ. I had no idea what that relationship meant at the time, but He has encouraged me toward relationships. I am friends with some of the smartest, most spiritual, weirdest, not-so-cool, most broken, bravest, not-so-brave, most successful, not-so-successful, most egotistical, most famous, richest, poorest, most beautiful, not-so-beautiful, most lovable, most contrary, young, middle-aged, and old people. A few you would recognize, but most you would not. I love them all. I learn from them all. I am thankful for them all.

Having grandchildren has justified my childlike thinking. All I have to do is be with them, and my mind races to heights of the wild, blue yonder. Oh the fun I have with them! Watching them play, hearing them laugh, hearing them say things that only make sense to them and me, and hearing them make up songs that must make God's heart leap is better than hearing a world-class symphony. As young as they are, I still learn so much from them. If you need a new spirit of creativity in your life, spend time talking with a child. I mean, have a real conversation. All you have to do is observe what they might be interested in and simply ask them a question. Then sit back and catch the brilliance.

Simple things recalibrate our hearts, and while those things are different for each of us, we must always be looking for them. A recalibrated heart causes mystery and curiosity. This is what I love about the devotions in *Reflect*. As I read these stories I hear music, I see things I haven't seen before. My imagination races, and my faith jumps up several notches.

The things we love to do now will eventually change. What you are doing now will sooner or later evolve to something different. In fact, sooner or later those things won't even exist. That gives us all the more reason to work hard at loving what we do. But when change comes, we can learn to love the new just as much as the familiar. I have reinvented myself several times. And now, in this season of life, certainly coaching and mentoring people are what I love most. But mentoring is different from coaching. For that matter, it's even different than teaching or training. Mentoring is "fathering," or putting your thumbprint on someone's life.

Reflect came from a scripture verse I love, Proverbs 27:19: "As water reflects the face, so one's life reflects the heart." The next

9

time you see a body of water that is completely still, think about how your life reflects your heart. A wonderful reminder! This mental picture of a calm body of water—one you can look into and see the trees and clouds reflected—also reminds us of God's beauty and His majesty. The thing I love the most, however, is the truth it teaches us about God's calmness and how He listens. When you experience this beauty, you will be calm and listen as well.

Welcome to *Reflect*.

Stan Endicott

1 ·········• EYE OF THE BEHOLDER

Rejoice in the Lord always. I will say it again: Rejoice! Let your gentleness be evident to all. The Lord is near. Do not be anxious about anything, but in every situation, by prayer and petition, with thanksgiving, present your requests to God. And the peace of God, which transcends all understanding, will guard your hearts and your minds in Christ Jesus. *(Philippians 4:4-7)*

Not long ago I had the wonderful opportunity to become acquainted with a National Geographic photographer. I saw some of his work on a DVD at a conference and was so inspired that I decided to take a risk and contact him through his web site. When you submit a comment or question through "contact us" on a web site, you don't really expect to hear from anyone. At least that's been my experience. Well, this time I was wrong. Way wrong.

Two days after I e-mailed the photographer he called my cell phone. I didn't recognize the number, but I answered anyway. I heard an unfamiliar voice say, "Stan, this is Dewitt Jones, the photographer from National Geographic." I was shocked! Dewitt went on to say he had received my e-mail and would like to meet with me. My original inquiry was about the processes he uses to generate creativity. (I believe all great creativity has a process, even though it might be a very loose one.) I couldn't wait to find out what made this guy click.

Dewitt invited a colleague of mine and me to have lunch with him. It was one of the most fascinating lunches I have ever had. We talked about family, careers, creativity, God, and culture. I came away convinced that highly skilled people take great care in gathering the right tools for their craft. But Dewitt reminded me that gifted people could accomplish amazing things, even if they don't have the finest tools available. During a lull in the conversation, I asked Dewitt if he could take beautiful pictures with a twelve-dollar, cardboard throwaway camera. "Of course I can," he answered. "It's all about the lighting, the angles, the timing, and the skill." What a great life lesson!

I love to observe people encountering God. What an amazing thing to experience! Dewitt's statement that he can take great pictures with an expensive Nikon or with a twelve-dollar cheapy reminded me that I need to be able to worship God in any situation. I don't need the best lighting, the best band, or the best anything to worship God. I can turn my heart toward Him in any circumstance.

The disposable camera has become an icon for my spiritual journey. When I see one on the shelf in the store or stuffed into someone's pocket or backpack, I am drawn to move my heart toward God. The beauty is not in the tools; the beauty is in the heart that uses them.

Today's Prayer

Lord, teach me how to worship you with all my heart. I want to stop allowing circumstances such as the quality of the music or the graphics on the screen or even the pacing of the service to "take me out." Create in me a heart of beauty. Amen.

Stan Endicott
Slingshot Group Partner
Worship Leader
Mariners Church, Irvine, CA

2 ·········• FOUR POWERFUL WORDS

Encourage one another and build each other up. *(1 Thessalonians 5:11)*
The tongue has the power of life and death. *(Proverbs 18:21)*

As a young man I had a mentor and friend named Otis Skillings. A gifted arranger, Otis was there to catch the first crest of the contemporary Christian music wave back in the late 1960s, and his work in both artist-driven and choir-driven Christian music was remarkable.

I first worked with Otis while traveling with the initial contemporary Christian music band by the unlikely name of The Spurrlows (a hybrid of the founder's name, Thurlow Spurr—another early giant). Otis was an arranger for the group, and he spent significant time with us in rehearsal camp and on the road teaching us the music he had arranged for us. To my everlasting benefit, we hit it off and developed a relationship that continued after I left the group two years later.

Otis taught me many things about music and arranging, and he demonstrated to me how to successfully walk the Christian life as a musician. I owe him much for those two things alone. But the greatest thing he ever did for me was to say these words over and over: "I believe in you." He said them in person. He said them over the phone. He wrote them on postcards while he was flying to London or somewhere else to record. And I desperately needed to hear them. I was a twenty-something, quite certain that I didn't possess whatever it took to succeed as a career musician. With those four words, he gradually changed my mind, and in so doing, my life.

Given Otis' example, and the scriptures I've listed above, I want to ask you this: What is it that you consistently communicate to those with whom you serve? Are you always looking for ways to assert your authority, or do you instead come alongside and encourage? Do you easily take umbrage at offenses, real or imagined, or are you quick to turn the other cheek and speak blessing? Do you walk in the realization that working with people, especially in worship ministry, is bound to be messy most of the time, and embrace that messiness as part of the job description? Words are meaningful to people, and the people behind the words are even more meaningful. What is your response when someone lets you down or disappoints you in some way? Is it to berate them, or even worse, to ignore the person and hope he or she will just go away? My friend, you have it within your power, through God's Spirit within you, to positively alter another's life by using four words and by showing with all you do and say that you mean them. You can lift people up, or you can squash them. It is to your advantage, to the health of the church, and to the glory of God, to lift them up. People will live up, or down, to your expectations of them. Teach them, train them, point out the error of their ways if necessary. But even then, speak the truth in love.

Today's Prayer

Dear Lord, help me to truly believe in people, to encourage someone today. Let my tongue be one that gives life. Amen.

Dave Williamson
Arranger, Speaker, Worship Leader
Author, *God's Singers—a Guidebook for the Worship Leading Choir in the 21st Century*

3 ·········• A DEEPER YEARNING

The Lord your God is with you, the Mighty Warrior who saves. He will take great delight in you, in his love he will no longer rebuke you, but will rejoice over you with singing. *(Zephaniah 3:17)*

A few years ago, my dad had a heart valve failure and was rushed to the hospital. After a "routine" valve repair on the morning of Good Friday, a serious complication developed that had the medical team rushing him back into emergency surgery that evening. I slept in the waiting room that night, not knowing what news the morning would bring.

Thankfully, he came through the crisis, and on Saturday, as he was coming out of anesthesia, I sat next to him in the hospital. His first words to me were, "I missed you." I smiled tearfully, as I knew he still had no idea of how much he had been through the day before. Then he did something that I will never forget. My father looked at me and said, "I just want to look at your face."

In that single moment with my father, I sensed his love for me in a way I had never experienced before. It was as if I knew, deep in my soul, the way he felt about me the day I was born—that it didn't matter what I became, it didn't matter what I did—the only thing that mattered was that I was his, *his son,* and that he saw me, and he loved me.

For most guys, and maybe for women too, there is a big part of us that just wants our dad to be proud of us. We spend a lot of time and energy working hard to make him proud—to hear the words "good job!" But under all that effort, I believe we really yearn for something even deeper: a rock-solid knowledge in our gut that we are our father's son, and he loves us, *no matter what.*

As an artist, musician, and worship leader, so much of my work flows from the desire to please the heart of my Heavenly Father—to hear "well done" from the audience of One. But I also sense a deeper yearning to hear my Father say, "I see you, I love you, you are mine!"

Today's Prayer

Father God, I know there are times when you aren't so much looking for a demonstration of my love as much as you just want me to sit with you and let you look at my face and rejoice in the fact that I am yours. Open my heart to receive that powerful, life-giving love as you sing over me. Help me lead others to your heart, where they, too, can know that you see them, you love them, and they belong to you. Amen.

Brian Mulder
Pastor of Worship and Arts
North Suburban Church, Deerfield, Illinois

4 ·········• UNEXPECTED SURPRISES

If you, then, though you are evil, know how to give good gifts to your children, how much more will your Father in heaven give good gifts to those who ask him! *(Matthew 7:11)*

One year after Christmas, I was waiting to board a flight when I sat down long enough to overhear the end of a conversation between two women. One woman, off to catch her own flight, commented to the other, "I'm so sorry for the recent loss of your husband and hope you have a good visit with your family." My heart sank as I couldn't help but feel compassion for the elderly woman who had lost her husband at Christmastime. Suddenly, whatever meetings or things I needed to get done were of little importance. This woman's loss put into perspective the many things of life that are really unimportant in the larger scheme of things.

Life brings many surprises. If you receive news of an unexpected job promotion, this is a good surprise. Perhaps an even greater surprise is if a loved one tells you that you are going to be a parent or grandparent. But why does it often take surprises that are not considered ideal for God to get our attention and call our focus back to the things that are truly important? Why did it take a lady in an airport terminal, commenting to another lady on the recent loss of her husband, to call my attention to more important things? The reality is that we often become more dependent and focused on God when we receive bad surprises than when we receive good ones. Why is that?

In the Old Testament, the Israelites fell into the same pattern. God had brought them out of captivity—good surprise. He parted a path through the Red Sea to escape Pharaoh's army—good surprise. And He promised to lead them to a land flowing with milk and honey called the Promised Land—great surprise. Yet despite all the good surprises God gave, the Israelites still lost focus. Even their leader, Moses, wasn't allowed to enter the Promised Land because he lost focus. If they had kept their minds on what was important, they would never have had to experience the bad surprises.

God wants our full attention, as His desire is to give good gifts. Sometimes, due to sin and a fallen world, we will experience unexpected surprises that are not enjoyable. But when we focus on His priorities and not our own, we find a life filled with true contentment. It's when we become wrapped up in the unimportant details of life that we often create unpleasant situations for ourselves. The ultimate gift God desires to give us is a relationship with Him in which we are so caught up in His presence that we forget about our own small details. In that intimate relationship, there is the surprise of eternal joy.

Today's Prayer

Father, thank you for giving gifts that allow my life to be focused more on you. Open my eyes to see what things I need to be focusing on at this time in life and what areas I need to release. I know it's easy to become distracted and lose sight of what's important in life, but you have created me to know you intimately through the power of the best gift of all, Jesus. May your presence sustain me in all areas and your grace overwhelm me to the depths of my soul. Thank you for being a God who loves me unconditionally. Amen.

David Brown
Worship Pastor
Tri-Village Christian Church, Pataskala, Ohio

5 ·········• WHAT ARE *YOU* LOOKING AT?

No doubt about it! God is good—good to good people, good to the
good-hearted. But I nearly missed it, missed seeing his goodness.
I was looking the other way, looking up to the people at the top,
envying the wicked who have it made, who have nothing to worry
about, not a care in the whole wide world. Pretentious with
arrogance, they wear the latest fashions in violence, pampered
and overfed, decked out in silk bows of silliness. They jeer, using
words to kill; they bully their way with words. They're full of hot air,
loudmouths disturbing the peace. People actually listen to them—
can you believe it? Like thirsty puppies, they lap up their words.
What's going on here? Is God out to lunch? Nobody's tending the
store. The wicked get by with everything; they have it made, piling up
riches. I've been stupid to play by the rules; what has it gotten me?
A long run of bad luck, that's what—a slap in the face every time
I walk out the door. If I'd have given in and talked like this, I would
have betrayed your dear children. Still, when I tried to figure it out,
all I got was a splitting headache . . . until I entered the sanctuary of
God. Then I saw the whole picture: The slippery road you've put them
on, with a final crash in a ditch of delusions. In the blink of an eye,

disaster! A blind curve in the dark, and—nightmare! We wake up and rub our eyes. . . . nothing. There's nothing to them. And there never was. When I was beleaguered and bitter, totally consumed by envy, I was totally ignorant, a dumb ox in your very presence. I'm still in your presence, but you've taken my hand. You wisely and tenderly lead me, and then you bless me. You're all I want in heaven! You're all I want on earth! When my skin sags and my bones get brittle, GOD is rock-firm and faithful. Look! Those who left you are falling apart! Deserters, they'll never be heard from again. But I'm in the very presence of GOD—oh, how refreshing it is! I've made Lord GOD my home. GOD, I'm telling the world what you do! *(Psalm 73, TM)*

Recently, when I was reading this psalm, it struck me in a new way that what we look at matters!

What you see depends on which direction you are looking. What you perceive and think about depends on what you are focused on. How critically important it is that we are looking in the right direction. We need to be looking at the greatness and goodness of God, not at what is happening around us and imagining we are missing out on something.

In today's world, especially the part of the globe where I live, it is very easy to be distracted by the perceived success of others and the glamour of new and cooler "stuff." I have to constantly be on my guard to not get caught "looking the other way," so to speak.

What we focus on shapes our whole outlook on life. When we enter the sanctuary of God (the place of worship and seeking God) we will begin to see the whole picture (v. 17). The security and peace of being in God's presence and in God's hands can never be matched by what we see looking the other way.

Today's Prayer

God, help me to focus on your goodness and greatness so I can experience true peace and wholeness. Amen.

Mark Cullen
Worship Pastor
Coast Hills Community Church
Aliso Viejo, California

6 ··········• LOVE PEOPLE

When the Lord takes pleasure in anyone's way, he causes their enemies to make peace with them. *(Proverbs 16:7)*

Throughout the years I have been asked many questions about ministry. Questions like: "How do I get into the ministry?" "What should I do with this person?" or "What should I do with that situation?" and so on.

I have not always given helpful advice—especially in the beginning—but now I can truly say there is one answer that covers a multitude of inquiries.

Love people.

Ministry is a challenge and certainly not for the weak of heart. One must be truly called in order to endure the long race that is at times tiring, surprising, joy-filled, discouraging, overwhelming, exciting, and yes . . . always satisfying.

While on this wonderful journey, we may at times lose our bearings because the darkness of our own ignorance can blind us. No matter what, though, we can always turn to love.

When you work at loving people, your efforts will be honored by the Lord. Though not an easy endeavor, loving others is the highest calling.

"For God so loved the world that he gave his one and only Son" (John 3:16).

"God is love" (1 John 4:8).

"Love is patient, love is kind" (1 Corinthians 13:4).

To love is to please God.

I opened this devotional with a scripture verse that reminds me to please God first, expecting no reward for that effort other than peace from even my enemy.

I want to encourage you to do the same today.

Seek the love of God to heal any wounds that might adjust your life's filter. Seek God's love to fill your heart when you are dealing with those difficult people who are, at present, a grain of sand in your oyster that will someday become a pearl. Seek the love of God when all things look impossible, because He alone has proven there is nothing He cannot and has not overcome. And lastly, seek the love of God to please Him in everything you do and everywhere you go. Then watch as even your enemies turn their heads in wonder.

Today's Prayer

Lord, fill my heart with the blessing of your love so that I may bless others with it. Amen.

Chariya Bissonette
Creative Arts Director
New Song Christian Fellowship
Laguna Niguel, California

7 ·········• A PARROT'S PERSPECTIVE

As for me, it is good to be near God. *(Psalm 73:28)*

They say that a mature green Amazon parrot has the intelligence of a two- to four-year-old child. I believe it. We inherited Popeye from a sweet elderly woman who could no longer care for him. At any particular moment, Popeye breaks into a rendition of "I'm Popeye the Sailor Man" (hence, the name). He imitates everything, even the lawnmower. He barks like our chocolate lab, laughs and giggles like an infant, and has perfected all the subtle nuances of his previous owner's horrible smoker's cough. He loves music, preferably in the key of F, and exuberantly sings like Pavarotti (complete with vibrato) when I play the piano or guitar. Most of the time, he is a joy to have around and makes me and my family laugh a lot.

Popeye craves attention, particularly from me. If I fail to immediately say hello when I get home from work, and scratch the back of his neck for a minute, he begins to bark like a dog.

Popeye also likes to insert himself into every telephone chat, every conversation at the dinner table, and every television program. It gets a little weird, even eerie at times, especially when guests are visiting.

If I'm outside, Popeye wants to be outside; if I'm in the garage, he wants to be in the garage. If he weren't confined to his cage, he would follow me around and do whatever was necessary to end up on my shoulder in order to be as close to my ear as possible. Popeye's favorite thing is to be with me.

I think that's how Jesus wants my relationship with Him to be. The Psalmist expressed it well when he wrote, "As for me, it is good to be near God" (Psalm 73:28). In Psalm 16:11, he also writes, "You will fill me with joy in your presence, with eternal pleasures at your right hand."

God has gone to great lengths to make it possible for me to communicate with Him, and He with me. What's even more amazing is the fact that He is genuinely interested in who I am and what I have to say. It is still sometimes hard to grasp that He actually likes being with me. He loves it when I clamor for His attention in prayer, or when I eagerly devour His Word in the hopes of hearing Him say something especially for me. He enjoys it when, like my silly green parrot, I break out in praise, no matter how boisterous or clumsy.

Today's Prayer

God, thank you for loving me. Thank you for feeding me. Thank you for spending time with me. Thank you for cleaning my cage. Amen.

Rick Founds
Songwriter/Worship Leader
Fallbrook Presbyterian Church
Fallbrook, California

8 ··········• DEATH OUTSIDE OUR DOORS

> As for you, you were dead in your transgressions and sins, in which you used to live when you followed the ways of this world and of the ruler of the kingdom of the air . . . But because of his great love for us, God, who is rich in mercy, made us alive with Christ even when we were dead in transgressions. *(Ephesians 2:1-2, 4)*

It was 4:45 A.M., well before the time I usually get up on Sunday mornings. My iPhone chirped as the screen flashed the number of a missed call. I soon learned of a fatal car accident that had taken place in the night. The crash site was located directly in front of our church campus. Upon arrival, I observed yellow police tape completely blocking off both sides of the road and the main entrances to the church. All of our congregation undoubtedly would be confronted with the accident as they were forced to detour to a more obscure entrance. The shear force of the crash had torn the automobile apart, littering our campus with metal and glass and human remains. In disbelief I watched as one officer removed a human appendage from our carefully manicured grass. Another officer chalked out scattered remains located on our asphalt driveway. The image I'd carry into our collective time of worship would be of four partially filled body bags on our church lawn. Death was uncomfortably present outside our doors as we gathered for worship.

The apostle Paul writes a very similar thought to the Ephesian church. He reminds the church that death constantly surrounds us. It's the norm. It's the way of things. It's in our workplaces, in our neighborhoods, and sometimes even on our mowed lawns. Yet it's being undone. God is up to something. It involves second chances. It's unusual, wonderful, incredible, miraculous. God is making us "alive with Christ." That morning, I watched hundreds of people pass through a literal death scene as they gathered together in worship. It served as an incredible picture of what happens every week in our churches. Our gatherings are more than chords, vocal riffs, and perfectly executed transitions. They are the picture of life emerging from death. This incredible gathering should inspire awe in us every time we have the privilege of witnessing it. As worship leaders, we have a front-row seat to the incredible work of Christ.

Today's Prayer

God, help me keep it real. Help me never lose the sense of awe when I see those who are alive in Christ emerge from the dead. When I sing about the new life you give, and when I lead others to sing, may I be deeply aware of how close death really is to each of us. May my worship carry not only conviction but also concern—concern for those who are right outside our door. Amen.

Andy Gridley
Worship Architect
Calvary Church
Los Gatos, California

9 ·········• THE CURVEBALL

Many are the plans in a person's heart, but it is the LORD**'s purpose that prevails.** *(Proverbs 19:21)*

love playing baseball—especially against players better than me, because they help me grow into a savvier player. At first it wasn't easy. I remember when I was nine years old and stood in the batter's box as a mountainous, post-pubescent twelve-year-old pitcher with a five o'clock shadow stared me down. As he hurled that wicked curveball, my knees buckled and I froze like a statue.

Now, as an artist, painting live at events, a similar chill runs up my spine when someone throws me a verbal curveball like, "Uh, we have a problem."

The first time I heard those words was the very first time I painted live outside of my own church many years ago. The Celebration Recovery conference venue was set up in a way that didn't allow me to organize my supplies onstage until right before I was to start painting. So, as the worship team kicked into their first song, I scrambled to get the paint cans open.

I had bought "oops" paint—marked down because it was mixed wrong at the paint store. My heart nearly went through my chest as I opened each incorrectly marked can to discover DayGlo colors!

With a quick prayer, I felt God impress on me that this was no accident. So, with no other options available, I started painting with the few normal colors I had. Then as the painting transformed, I began to apply the bright colors and was soon throwing the paint at the canvas in an almost cathartic expression.

You see, the conference theme was about God giving everyone a new name, just as God gave Jacob the name Israel. All around me were people nailing—loudly and emotionally—their new names to crosses at the foot of the stage as I threw paint at an image of the Cross symbolizing the bright new lives these people had through Jesus' sacrifice.

It completely changed the way I painted. Formerly, I restricted myself with a timid and limited color palette. Now I don't hesitate to be expressive with my colors—bright or somber—whatever the subject matter dictates.

That first conference experience revealed to me that God, like a good baseball coach, sometimes throws us curveballs because, if it were up to us, we would cruise along just swinging at fastballs down the middle, and we would never improve. But when the curveballs force us out of our comfort zones and things get tough, God, our encouraging coach, whispers in our ears, "Trust your instincts, kid. I know you can do it."

My response now is, "Bring it!"

Today's Prayer

Lord, thank you that you are in every moment, especially those of discomfort and stress. Help me trust in you and allow your Spirit to flow through me. Help me lean into you when situations don't go as planned and to realize that problems with my plan may mean that you have a better plan. All I need to do is listen. Amen.

Tom Clark
Worship Artist
Tom Clark Studio
Capistrano Beach, California

10 ······• CAN YOU HEAR ME NOW?

Guard your steps when you go to the house of God. Go near to listen rather than to offer the sacrifice of fools, who do not know that they do wrong. Do not be quick with your mouth, do not be hasty in your heart to utter anything before God. God is in heaven and you are on earth, so let your words be few. *(Ecclesiastes 5:1-2)*

My kids sometimes say and do the most profound things. A few years ago, my three-year-old son came sneaking down the hallway toward my wife and me after we had put him to bed for the night. This wasn't necessarily an unusual occurrence, but this time we noticed he had his fingers in his ears. When we asked him why he was out of bed and why he was plugging his ears, he gave this matter-of-fact reply: "So I don't hear you when you tell me to go back to bed."

Seemed pretty ingenious, actually. He figured he could be present with us but avoid correction if he couldn't hear us speaking to him. The parallels to the life of a worshiper are obvious. How often do we desire to be in our Father's presence but have no interest in hearing what He has to say to us? We confidently saunter into His presence with fingers firmly planted into the ears of our hearts. We sense and enjoy our proximity with God, but we skillfully avoid having to hear and obey.

Jesus once asked His closest followers this piercing question: "Why do you call me, 'Lord, Lord,' and do not do what I say?" (Luke 6:46). True worship that God accepts is inseparable from true discipleship. And the biblical pattern for encountering the Living God always results in transformational implications for our lives (consider Job, Abraham, Moses, Isaiah, Paul, John, etc.).

Many of the psalms contain the cry "Lord, hear my voice," pleading for God to listen. It is, of course, all good and proper for us to expect God to listen to what we have to say to Him in worship—He delights in it and in us! But let's not forget that God also speaks into *our* lives. Jesus tells us that He is the Good Shepherd and His sheep hear His voice (John 10).

So, "Let the message of Christ dwell among you richly . . . through psalms, hymns, and songs from the Spirit, singing to God with gratitude in your hearts" (Colossians 3:16).

Today's Prayer

Father, we live noisy, distracted lives. And we often come before you slow to hear but quick to speak. Teach us, please, to be still before you, to remove the fingers from our ears, and to allow you to transform our lives according to your good pleasure and will. Jesus, we are your sheep, and we know and hear your voice. We desire to not just call you "Lord, Lord," but also to do what you say. Thank you for your grace and patience. Amen.

Jim Mitchell
Pastor for Worship
The Chapel, Akron, Ohio

11 ⋯⋯• BREATHLESS EXPECTATION

For this reason I kneel before the Father . . . I pray that out of his glorious riches he may strengthen you with power through his Spirit in your inner being, so that Christ may dwell in your hearts through faith. And I pray that you, being rooted and established in love, may have power, together with all the Lord's holy people, to grasp how wide and long and high and deep is the love of Christ, and to know this love that surpasses knowledge—that you may be filled to the measure of all the fullness of God. Now to him who is able to do immeasurably more than all we ask or imagine, according to his power that is at work within us, to him be glory in the church and in Christ Jesus throughout all generations, for ever and ever! Amen. *(Ephesians 3:14, 16-21)*

One summer our family was able to break away from our daily responsibilities and spend some time in Canada. We explored Quebec City and the surrounding mountains. It was an awesome combination: We alternated between spending days in a city vibrant with arts, culture, and unique experiences to experiencing the spectacular scenery and vistas where the Laurentian Mountains meet the St. Lawrence River.

Slowing down substantially and renewing our focus on God and family created the space in our lives for daily experiences that consistently took our breath away. Whether it was a hike through a canyon of dramatic waterfalls, the energy of streets filled with artists, the adrenaline rush of diving into a cold mountain river, or simply playing Uno with the family, each day was vibrant with life, relationships, and a sense of wonder.

Returning to ministry at the start of the following ministry season, I felt that same rush of excitement and anticipation. The rehearsals and services those first weeks were full of a dramatic sense of both God's presence and our hunger. It was great to be home. With my spirit fully dilated to the activity of God around me, I was blown away by the wildly creative ways God chose to move among us.

While every day certainly cannot be a mountaintop experience, each one can be approached with a sense of wonder and awe as we anticipate with breathless expectation how God might work in our lives, whether in big or small ways.

May we approach each day, each rehearsal, each conversation with expectation and faith, both of which involve a degree of uncertainty but also far exceed what we could manufacture in and of ourselves.

Today's Prayer

Lord, nudge my soul that I might embrace a life of faith and choose complete dependence on you. May I surrender my heart to the work you are doing in me. And may I love others so deeply that a wellspring of that love spills out in abundance toward the community of faith around me and beyond. Amen.

Chuck Spong
Executive Pastor of the Arts and Compassion
Winston-Salem First Assembly of God
Winston-Salem, North Carolina

12 ········• THE SOUND OF SILENCE

> My heart is not proud, oh Lᴏʀᴅ, my eyes are not haughty; I do not concern myself with great matters or things too wonderful for me. But I have stilled and quieted my soul; like a weaned child with its mother, like a weaned child is my soul within me. O Israel, put your hope in the Lᴏʀᴅ both now and forevermore. *(Psalm 131)*

I am not a strong swimmer. I grew up in inner-city Los Angeles, and most of my early experiences with bodies of water consisted of the pool at the local city park. My wife, Andi, on the other hand, grew up on a massive lake surrounded by mountains in western Montana. She spent most of her summers diving, swimming, playing—living in waters hundreds of feet deep. I tell you this because no matter how many times I've been there now, I can't seem to escape the anxiety and panic I feel when I jump into this monstrous lake. I can't quickly dog-paddle to the edges or grab for a handrail, and my feet never touch the safety of that wonderful concrete floor that bounces me back to the surface in seconds. I have no security whatsoever. I feel completely helpless, vulnerable, and out of control.

I felt something similar to that a few years ago while standing before a large crowd and leading a worship service. The band was going strong, the room was filled with hands lifted high as together we proclaimed the words of adoration displayed before us on a jumbo screen. And then we felt compelled to take a risk.

The music gradually stopped. The screen went dark, and one by one the team began to kneel in silence.

I felt a strong sense of anxiety emerge in what had just moments earlier been an electrical, tangible wave of energy in the room.

Granted, there can be a right way, a wrong way, even a manipulative way to do this. Our spirits, however, felt united in proceeding this way in an act that was neither premeditated nor disruptive. Why, then, so much tension?

Our culture devalues silence. Studies have shown that if there is more than fifteen seconds of silence in a group, someone will speak. Even in worship we often devalue or become uncomfortable with silence, choosing to fill every second with music or speech.

What is it about silence that we find so frightening? Is it in silence that we may be confronted with our greatest fears, doubts, or personal demons?

Is it possible that in the midst of all our worship and singing we have neglected to leave room for God to respond and for us to listen to his still, small voice?

What would it look like if we were not only comfortable but also deliberate about worshiping God in the midst of sheer silence?

As I think back on my need for familiarity and security when plunging into the lake, it begs me to ask myself, *Is it necessary for me to have the security of guided words and music to be able to worship God?*

Think of some of the familiar phrases we sing during our corporate worship: "When the music fades . . . all is stripped away. . . . and I simply come . . . And it's your beauty, Lord, that makes us stand in silence. . . ."

How often do we do that—let the music fade—stand in silence?

Of course, there are times for shouting, dancing with joy, or whispering His name. But could it be that at times the most appropriate response is to be still and know that He is God?

It seems the very thought of God in His majesty and holiness should silence us! The prophet Habakkuk declares, "But the Lord is in His holy temple; let all the earth be silent before Him" (Habakkuk 2:20).

I invite you to dare to allow yourself to spend some time in silence and listen for the voice of God. Inwardly ask the Holy Spirit to allow you to hear God's voice.

Today's Prayer

Teach me to stand in awed silence before you, Lord, waiting and listening. Amen.

Carlos Fernandez
Worship Leader
Saintfield, Northern Ireland

13 ⋯⋯• THROUGH A GLASS DARKLY

Now we see only a reflection as in a mirror; then we shall see face to face. Now I know in part; then I shall know fully, even as I am fully known. *(1 Corinthians 13:12)*

It was an incredible serve. After countless misfires, the law of averages finally owed me one great one. With an explosion of energy I sent a little blue ball screaming off the front wall, inches off the ground, and diving for the extreme backhand corner. In my mind I had the point won before I ever turned around. I knew that there was no way Terry would even touch it!

But Terry doesn't give up that easily. Arms and legs were flying everywhere as I turned to admire my work. And by some miracle of chance his racket actually hit the ball. Straight at my face.

In the next instant I learned how age slows your reflexes. Before I even thought about reacting I found myself on the floor clutching my left eye. Aside from being extremely painful, one thing was immediately evident: I couldn't see anything past the right side of my nose.

That was the beginning of a scary week. After reaching the locker room, I found that the pupil of my left eye was half-filled with blood. Doctors talked of internal bleeding and sticking needles in my eye to drain it. Others considered surgery. The most lasting and important effect of all this, though, was that I still couldn't see. At least not really.

Have you ever tried looking through waxed paper? Try combining three or four sheets and looking through it. That will give you a good idea of what things looked like to me. I had never spent much time thinking about my sight, but suddenly all I knew was that I desperately wanted to see things clearly again. And my greatest fear was that I would spend the rest of my days seeing only the vague images of life around me.

And yet, in a very real way, the apostle Paul tells me that is exactly how I do see. When it comes to seeing things beyond the physical realm, he tells me I "see through a glass, darkly" (1 Corinthians 13:12, KJV). As hard as I squint at spiritual things, the best I can see are vague shapes of what is real.

That is why Paul prayed that the eyes of our hearts would be enlightened. The same man who wrote that, for now, we only see a poor reflection—and who told us that we walk by faith and not by sight—also prayed we would learn to see. He understood what it meant to look through damaged eyes. He knew that sin and the pressures of life would ensure most of us only see the dim outlines of the crisp wonders that are ours in Christ. Yet he also knew that over time, as we seek Him with all our hearts, His power and glory can come more clearly into focus. He prayed that we would see Jesus.

My eye slowly improved. Gradually, little by little, blobs became shapes, and blurred edges became clearer. In time my eye healed, and now I can see just fine. Sometimes I sense there's been healing in the eyes of my heart as well. Every now and then, when I'm quiet, when I'm yielded, when I truly seek His face, I find that I can just begin to make out some of the letters on the next line down on the wall.

That is why I love to worship. For in worship we see Jesus. In worship, we seek Him with all our hearts. And while we worship, He shows us just a little more of who He truly is. For just a moment He opens our eyes and restores our sight, and He gives us a brief glimpse of what it will be to someday see Him face-to-face.

Today's Prayer

Lord Jesus, I long to see you more clearly, to understand the breadth and length and depth of your glory and love. Open the eyes of my heart today so that I might know you more.

Joe Horness
Programming Director/Worship Leader
Bay Pointe Community Church
Traverse City, Michigan

14 ⋯⋯• LOSS HAPPENS

> So I find this law at work: Although I want to do good, evil is right there with me. For in my inner being I delight in God's law; but I see another law at work in me, waging war against the law of my mind and making me a prisoner of the law of sin at work within me. What a wretched man I am! Who will rescue me from this body that is subject to death? Thanks be to God, who delivers me through Jesus Christ our Lord! *(Romans 7:21-25)*

This verse is encouraging to me. Here we have the apostle Paul, the greatest evangelist of all time, admitting that he has the same struggle with sin that I do. "What a wretched man I am!" Mind-boggling.

There's a Van Morrison song titled "I'm Tired Joey Boy" that describes a lot of what I feel as a musician, with high mountaintops one year and deep, dark valleys the next.

One of the verses caught my ear the first time I heard it because it says exactly what my life as a musician has been for decades—following my ambition to be someone, to make my mark, and let people see my God-given talent. But when I follow that to an extreme it has sometimes gotten me into trouble. So then I begin to go to the other extreme by completely shutting off the "me," as it were, to the point that I pretty much lose my identity as a musician and as a person.

When I look at the life of Jesus, it's different from my own experience. I want to be like Christ the teacher: the wise master, the miracle worker, the compassionate healer. Yet I also want to be the courageous Christ: the righteous, fiery Jesus who threw out the money changers, confronted the self-righteous Pharisees, and healed on the Sabbath. Here is the only human in history who lived a perfect, sinless life. He had no self-ambition, always set the perfect example, and always said and did the right thing. But I don't come anywhere near what Jesus was like.

I've experienced a great deal of loss in the last year. I lost my grandma, important relationships, my job of twelve years, and I almost lost my life in a car accident. I'm still recovering from that. I'm not saying these things because I want sympathy, but because I've seen God work in some amazing ways. My two boys were recently baptized and confessed Jesus as their Lord and Savior. I've been praying for that for years. The fact that I'm writing this right now is a testament of God's grace and power.

Maybe you've been going through a "loss year" as well. Maybe you've made some mistakes, or maybe bad things have happened over which you had no control. In the midst of it all, we can be confident that in this body of flesh—that carries with it sin and death—Jesus is working through us. Thanks be to God through His Son Jesus Christ!

Today's Prayer

> *Lord, some of us have suffered great loss, lost a loved one or a close relationship. Carry us through the hard, dark times and let us know for certain that it's you holding us tightly in your arms. Amen.*

Dave Thrush
Recording Artist
Faith Bible Chapel International
Aurora, Colorado

15 ⸱⸱⸱⸱⸱⸱⸱• YOU LOOK FAMILIAR

For those God foreknew he also predestined to be conformed to the image of his Son, that he might be the firstborn among many brothers and sisters. *(Romans 8:29)*

It always happens right in the middle of leading worship: my cell phone starts vibrating. I've learned to ignore it and keep playing, but it always feels funny. One particular morning after we finished playing, I walked off the platform to the back room, put my guitar down, and checked the messages. There was one from Dad. "Son, it's your grandma. The doctor doesn't give her much time. Your mom just left to be with her. I thought you would want to know."

I folded up the phone and packed up my equipment, but instead of going in to listen to the sermon, I headed to the airport. It was a long trip to western South Dakota with a couple of connecting flights along the way.

I arrived in the darkened intensive care unit room around one o'clock in the morning. Grandma, both tired and groggy from the pain meds, looked up warily at me and said she wasn't ready to "leave" just yet. Not sure what she meant, I walked closer to give her a kiss. When my face came into view she cried, "Oh my, little Doug, I thought you were Jesus; I was surprised that He'd be coming personally." My family still laughs to this day at how with my long hair and the dim lights Grams mistook me for Jesus. She did stay and visit with us for a few days longer, then left to be with Jesus on Thanksgiving morning.

There are debates today among churches about whether worship should be led by paid professionals or by volunteers. There are those who want their worship facilities to have all the latest bells and whistles, and others who want them to be simple and stripped down. Other debates arise as to whether we should use progressive, contemporary, emergent, liturgical, acoustic, electric, alternative, missional, blended, ancient-future, or traditional styles of worship. And I would say to all of this emphatically: Yes! It's all good! Or sadly, no, none of it is any good. What makes the difference is whether or not the congregation mistakes us for Jesus.

It all boils down to the heart. This is something no one can fake. There's no "Jesus" mask we can put on. If we're not right with Him, the whole place notices. It's His stage. Jesus deserves the best effort and the best preparation we can offer. Honor Him when it's just the two of you, and there will be far less attention on you when there's a crowd.

Today's Prayer

Lord, don't let me get in the way. Don't let people see me; let them see only you. Help me remember that anything of value in me comes from you. I'm so thankful Grams finally got to see you face-to-face. I'm looking forward to that, too. Amen.

Doug Olson
DMA Candidate/Indiana University Jacobs School of Music
Worship Leader
Indianapolis, Indiana

16 ········• BIRTHDAYS

So the man went away and began to tell in the Decapolis how much
Jesus had done for him. And all the people were amazed. *(Mark 5:20)*

Our worship gatherings are a lot like birthday parties, or at least
they should be. Let me give an example.

Imagine it's my son's birthday and family members have gathered from all over the country to celebrate. My wife leads everyone
in singing "Happy Birthday," and a cake appears as the chorus
fills the house. Candles are glowing and dripping wax on the cake
we're about to consume. Everyone is loving it. This is a big deal.
Their joy at being able to watch our son grow and be a part of his
wonderful, beautiful life for the past year is now overflowing in loud
song and wide smiles. However, something is amiss. People begin
to awkwardly notice that I, the father, am just standing there with
my arms folded . . . not singing.

After the moment of focused celebration has passed and people begin to mingle while eating cake, my brother-in-law corners me
and says, "Dude, you weren't singing." In other words, "What's your
problem?" I then reply, "Well, there are a few reasons. First, singing

really isn't my thing. I show my love for Judah (my son) in other ways. Second, my wife started off the song in a key that was too low for me. Third, my wife and I had a small argument today, and I just couldn't follow her song leadership and sing with sincerity."

If that really happened, I would hope that my brother-in-law would respond with, "Are you serious? Get over yourself!" after picking his jaw up off the floor due to shock at my cluelessness.

As a worship and song leader, this is an easy connection for me to make—and easy for me to say since singing is somewhat part of my job. Yet even if singing were not "my thing," it is a part of what God has called me to do. And I love to thank God because He saved my life, created me and chose me to be in relationship with Him and pursued my redemption. I can't help but sing and shout and tell. I love to praise Him because of who He is.

One last word: part of what makes "Happy Birthday" renditions so wonderful is that they usually do sound bad, but people still go for it with gusto. It's a wonderful sight: friends and family celebrating with joy and loudness, unashamed.

Today's Prayer

May God give us the wisdom to not criticize but lovingly exhort our congregations to sing of their love for Him. May we, like the man in Mark 5, simply tell, sing, and shout of what Jesus has done for us in such a way that those with ears to hear are amazed and sing along, not out of guilt, but with a common love. Amen.

Martin Allen, President
Worship Foundations International
<www.worshipfoundations.com>
Los Angeles, California

17 ········• I KNOW THIS FULL WELL

I praise you because I am fearfully and wonderfully made; your works are wonderful, I know that full well. *(Psalm 139:14)*

When I look back on my childhood, and even part of my teenage years, much of what I remember is sitting in the waiting rooms of many different doctors' offices. I remember wishing I wasn't there and thinking that I really didn't need to be there. I never expressed this to the doctors, but I'm sure they would have disagreed. I grew up with a severe learning disability, and I was prescribed the highest dose of medication to treat my disorder. But even that wasn't enough. Doctors told me I would never move on to the next grade in school without at least failing it once. They also told me I wouldn't be able to participate in normal dialogue and that public speaking would be too difficult for me to handle—ever. Because of my disability I was given extra help in school and more time to take my tests. I know all the extra care was meant to help, and it did, but I still hated it. I always felt inferior to my schoolmates and friends. As a result I had very low self-esteem. I certainly didn't realize that God was allowing all of this to happen so that my life would later reflect His glory.

When David wrote Psalm 139:14 you can tell he was in a time of reflection. He had already beaten Goliath. He was already victorious in war, and he held the highest rank there was: he was the king. Even though he was already victorious and well-accomplished, he had no idea of the legacy his life would leave. He had no idea that we would be reading his psalms and his life's story. He had no idea that the Son of God would be identified as the "Son of David." He had no idea that all these years later he would still be so famous. David started off as a shepherd but ended as a victor, a worship leader, a psalmist, and a king. From the time he was just a shepherd to the time he was king, David was always one thing, whether or not he saw it: fearfully and wonderfully made.

If you had told me when I was a child that I was fearfully and wonderfully made, I probably wouldn't have bought into it. But I am finally at a place now that I understand and believe it. I know that I was pieced together by God and that all He does He does well. Those doctors weren't wrong for diagnosing me as they did, but I'm so glad God spoke over their diagnoses and brought me to where I am now. Despite any doctor's words, I never failed a grade or was left behind. I graduated college and now speak publicly more often than most. I am the youth pastor of a great ministry called Youth Explosion in New York City. I have learned one thing from my life, as well as from the life of David, and that is when you are a worshiper, it doesn't matter how the world sees you or what the world calls you. Worshipers hear the voice of God in the lonely sheep pastures and dark waiting rooms. They hear Him saying, "You are not what they tell you. You are fearfully and wonderfully made."

Today's Prayer

Lord, thank you for doing all things well. I give you thanks for what you do in my life. Let me see myself as you see me, fearfully and wonderfully made. Amen.

Chris Durso
Director of Youth Explosion Ministries
Christ Tabernacle
Glendale, New York

18 ········• GAZING VERSUS GLANCING

> You, God, are my God, earnestly I seek you; I thirst for you, my body
> longs for you, in a dry and parched land where there is no water. I
> have seen you in the sanctuary and beheld your power and your glory.
> Because our love is better that life, my lips will glorify you. *(Psalm
> 63:1-3)*

The year was one of the busiest. The church was growing, worship services were being added, and there was a quick pace of positive change. All the things you would hope to see in ministry were happening as far as numbers, quality, and depth of worship volunteers. Years of planning, prayer, and hard work were all paying off. Now it was finally time to take a family vacation.

My wife booked us a two-room cottage on Gold Beach on the southern coast of Oregon. The rustic and simple structure was not meant to do anything other than blend in with the surroundings. From the top of the bluff, our front porch overlooked an unobstructed view of the beach and the Pacific Ocean. I was awestruck by the sunset the first night and knew that I would end each day on our porch quietly gazing at the horizon as the colors changed from yellows to oranges to purples to gray.

On that first night I took pictures, video, and even journaled about my experience in real time. The surprise of what I was feeling caught my attention, and my reaction was to capture it rather than experience it. I was not moved by all the extra activity; it took me from a gaze to a glance. Worship of God is not about stolen glances but about my intentional gaze.

Once I put away my things, something began to happen. I felt a release. I heard the waves and smelled the sea. My mind began to clear. I was actually talking to God, and somehow the surrounding natural colors, shapes, and gentle breeze reached out to me. The longer I soaked it in, the more I could feel at peace in my body, soul, and mind.

Ending each afternoon this way drew me into the experience in a deeper way. My shoulders loosened from the stress of being on task at my church ministry. My mind quieted enough for me to thoughtfully read a book I was hoping to finish. We played family board games with little arguing. And my soul grew space to listen and experience the present moments.

When we actually gaze at true beauty we never seem to tire of its effect. However, distractions prove to be limitless with the constant onslaught of digital images and messages from our smart phones and other tethered devices. Our work life, social life, and even our spiritual life can be lived virtually.

I love technology and believe that just as printing technology allowed God's Word to spread, smart phones and the Internet will reach people in unprecedented ways both today and in the future.

Even so, the practice of repeatedly gazing into the beauty of God needs a place. The breathtaking sunset each night taught me that God's beauty is right in front of me. Becoming still enough to view Him this way takes my undivided focus.

We cannot bottle up the mountaintop experiences or the beachside epiphanies to relive them, but we surely should find and plan for a way to gaze at our God in all His glory. In doing so, His beauty will change us.

Today's Prayer

Dear God, help me lose my distractions and keep my focus on you. Let me be successful in planning times and places to gaze at your beauty, listen to your voice, and be changed by the encounter. Amen.

Rich Kirkpatrick
Worship Leader/Blogger
RKWeblog.com & worshipmythbusters.com
Murrieta, California

19 ·······• I WILL AWAKEN THE DAWN

Awake, my soul! Awake, harp and lyre! I will awaken the dawn.
I will praise you, Lord, among the nations; I will sing of you
among the peoples. *(Psalm 57:8-9)*

It was the hour just before first light. Our makeshift village at the
Varkiza campground on the shores of the Aegean Sea near Athens was still quiet as most of the Youth With A Mission (YWAM)
campers slept. We were approximately two hundred Discipleship
Training School (DTS) students and staff from about fifteen nations. We had come to Greece to share the love of Christ. I was
very excited to be in this historic land where the apostle Paul had
preached about the "unknown god" on Mars Hill. We would be
celebrating Easter on that very spot in a few days.

In the midst of this awesome spiritual experience, however,
the everyday realities of life were foremost on my mind. I had not
been able to get a shower in five days! There were four showers for
one hundred women, and the lines were long most of the day. My

first thought was *surely if I get up before dawn I can get a shower.* I jumped out of my sleeping bag, grabbed my towel, shampoo, and soap and rushed to the concrete showers. But there *was* a line. I decided instead to take another "spit bath" and go up on the hill overlooking the camp and enjoy the sunrise over the sea with the Lord.

The sunrise was spectacular! I had such a sense of calling and mission as I watched the Lord create the day. I had been learning how to "sing a new song" to the Lord. Although I had been a Christian concert artist for years, I was discovering the joy of singing just for my Heavenly Father. An audience of One! My soul was being filled once again with the power of God's love. This was the equipping I needed, as we would be venturing out into the city with our music and dramas that afternoon. At that moment, though, it wasn't about equipping, it was about being in God's presence, connected to eternity.

As I boldly sang out, "Lord, I'll go anywhere for you," I stopped. Do I *really* mean that? The next day one of my new Dutch friends would be leaving to work at a refugee camp in Thailand. It was dangerous there. We would often pray for the safety of our YWAMers and the refugees as we heard regular reports of attacks along the Thai-Cambodian border. Would I be willing to *die* serving others for God's sake? As I paused and pondered this thought, the Lord spoke clearly to my heart: *The power that you are feeling now is the same no matter where I lead you. The safest place you will ever be is in my will and in my presence. Whenever you are feeling weak, get up early, watch a sunrise, and draw from my strength again.* I have now done that many times over the four decades I have been in ministry. I *know* I am always safe in Him.

Today's Prayer

Lord, may each new sunrise remind me that you are my strength. You are my safe place. Amen.

Karen Lafferty
Writer of "Seek Ye First"
Director of Youth With A Mission
Santa Fe/Musicians for Missions International
Santa Fe, New Mexico

20 ......• EVER BEEN SCARED OF THE DARK?

Even though I walk through the darkest valley, I will fear no evil, for you are with me; your rod and your staff, they comfort me.
(Psalm 23:4)

When I was kid I was scared of the dark, just like every other kid my age. I remember lying in bed at night, imagining the boogieman sleeping under my bed, just waiting in the dark to get me. It messed with my mind so much that I would yell for my dad in the other room to come save me. Of course, like any other dad, he came running into the room telling me there was nothing there and to go back to sleep. However, one night he had finally had enough. He came in my room after I had cried *again* about the boogieman, threw back the covers, and told me to get under the bed. He told me I was going to have to sleep under the bed to learn there was nothing there. Then he went back to his room, got his pillow, and crawled under my bed with me. We both slept there together. I never worried about the boogieman after that night.

There is a great metaphor in this story for how we live our spiritual lives. The *darkness* in this story represents many things. It represents evil in this world. It represents the unknown, the mysterious, the things outside of our control. It represents the work of the devil. *Fear* in this story represents uncertainty and doubt. It represents a lack of faith. Looking through this metaphorical lens, I learned several things about my spiritual life from my dad in this experience. One is that we don't have to be scared of the "dark." The Bible tells us in Colossians 1:13, "For he has rescued us from the dominion of darkness and brought us into the kingdom of the Son he loves." As followers of Jesus Christ, too many times we live our lives scared of the darkness—scared of the unknown and the things we can't see. We forget we are free as children of the King. We have no need to wonder who is in control . . . no need to position ourselves in what we think is a safe place. We need only to trust. And when we trust—when we have faith—we are free to take risks, and taking risks for the building of the Kingdom here on earth should be in our DNA at all times. I also learned that God never leaves us alone. He goes into the darkness with us. In fact, darkness runs from Him. In 1 John 1:5-7 we read, "This is the message we have heard from him and declare to you: God is light; in him there is no darkness at all. If we claim to have fellowship with him and yet walk in the darkness, we lie and do not live out the truth. But if we walk in the light, as he is in the light, we have fellowship with one another, and the blood of Jesus, his Son, purifies us from all sin."

If the boogieman was there before my dad and I climbed under the bed, he was gone by the time we got there. I've found that to be true in more ways than one. When I step out in faith with God,

He goes before me. He is the light pushing back the darkness. This experience has renewed me several times as a worship leader. I remember I am not alone. God always goes before me, and there is nothing that can stop Him and me from accomplishing His will in this world. So let's trust Jesus as our Savior, our Deliverer, and our Friend. Have faith, take a risk, get under the bed!

Today's Prayer

Lord, as we stand for you in a dark and scary world, we find comfort and courage in knowing you stand with us. Amen.

Kyle Dillard
Worship Arts Director
Lake Forest Church
Huntersville, North Carolina

21 ·········• BEING STILL

Be still, and know that I am God. *(Psalm 46:10)*

Reading this verse immediately makes me think of things that bring me comfort, like my favorite T-shirt or scone paired with a great cup of coffee. This is so familiar. I know I see it at least once a month on a card, in a book, or cross-stitched on one thing or another.

As much as I have seen and heard this verse and think I understand it, why do I find it so difficult to be still? Why is it that when I finally sit down to connect with the Lord it feels as if it's been eons since the last time? And why is it that when I attempt to quiet my mind in the "stillness," I find my mind in an entirely different place after about two-and-half minutes?

I have finally come to the realization that my lack of trust and the need to have control will always be the reason I can't seem to clear my head of all that has to get done. I have also come to realize that this is like working out. The more I do it, the easier it becomes. My pastor passed along an amazing tool to use during our quiet times. Although I have never been one who gets excited about journaling, it keeps me focused and removes distraction from my mind.

Thirty minutes that can change your life:

Ten minutes—Yesterday: What you did (decisions, feelings, observations)

Physical/Emotional/Spiritual

"An unexamined life is not worth living."

Ten minutes—God's Word (Psalm 119:11, 105)

Write: observations, thoughts, and insights

Ten minutes—Adoration (Who is God and what is He doing?)

Confession (being honest with God)

Thanksgiving (What has He done that I am thankful for?)

Supplication (What are my requests?)

That's it. Sometimes I don't even get past the first ten-minute prompt! The important thing is that, as a worship leader, I am always striving to create space during a service for the audience to connect through music and "take inventory" individually.

If I, the worship leader, have not taken the time to do my own personal inventory, I am coming to the table disconnected. It is much harder to walk my audience through something I have not even had time to do myself!

"Be still, and know that I am God" commands me to be at peace with whatever is in my life. It will always be difficult, but He has promised He will walk me through it. That's all I need for today.

Today's Prayer

Lord, help me always find time to be alone with you. Help me listen for and recognize your voice as you lead me. Amen.

Kim Johnson
Worship Leader
Mariners Church
Irvine, California

22 ·········• SLAYING THE DRAGON OF DUPLICITY

Such a person is double-minded, and unstable in all they do.
(James 1:8)

I'm sure my second-grade teacher, Ms. Morgan, wouldn't mind me mentioning this. She never intended to make my life difficult by telling Mom that I would be a jack-of-all-trades and master of none. Truth is, I latched on to that pronouncement as though she were conferring knighthood upon me. Perhaps I was just too young to foresee the battles I'd be facing as a result of accepting this "title." I simply didn't understand that I was about to be engaged in an epic struggle with the dragon of duplicity.

I was only seven years old when I first heard those fateful words: jack-of-all-trades. The Beatles had made their first appearance on the Ed Sullivan Show, and the rock and roll bug had already bitten me—badly. Soon I was passionately flailing my first guitar. In my childish estimation, being a jack-of-all-trades held some mysterious promise that maybe I could be good at all things musical. I intended to learn to play every instrument and sing every part in the band. For that matter, I wholeheartedly believed I would become an expert at each.

It never happened. What developed instead was the type of frustration that is commonly seen in those who wander without clear direction. I was struggling to do too many things at once and trying to be excellent at every one. I groped along this life-path for many years, never considering that if I just zeroed in on a single discipline I might finally reach that level of excellence I so deeply desired.

It was a sunny Sunday in east Texas in 1993 when the Lord finally broke the chains of my musical multi-perfectionism. During the morning service, He clearly spoke to my heart and said that I was no longer to be a jack-of-all-trades and master of none. He set me free from the dungeon of misdirection and instructed me forever to focus on one mission: *To go before His throne and take others with me.* I finally had a clear path to follow for the rest of my life. From that day forward, everything I set my hand to would be prioritized and measured by His specific will for me.

Fought any good dragons lately? Getting a clear understanding of life direction doesn't have to be as difficult as a medieval battle with an overgrown lizard. It can be as simple as answering a couple of foundational questions about ourselves. *Who am I? What am I doing?* Fortunately, these questions apply to any area of life that needs a bit of compass correction. Ultimately, our answers can be crafted into a simple mission statement, designed to be referred to again and again. Whenever life begins to look like a maze of rabbit trails, having a clear, concise mission statement can save you time, energy, and backtracking.

In order to avoid the instability spoken of in James 1:8, we should seek after life answers based on biblical principles. Properly applied, these will empower us to stay focused on God's specific will and direction for the long haul. When our solid, personal mission statement finally emerges, it becomes a life-changing, fruit-producing tool. Remember, if you don't know where you're going, any road will get you there!

Today's Prayer

Lord, keep my feet on a singular path, always traveling in your direction. Open doors for me that no man can close, and close the doors that lead in any way but yours. Amen.

Sandy Hoffman
Worship Leader/Trainer
Grace Community Church
Santa Fe, New Mexico
<www.EssentialWorship.com>

23 ·········• THEY HAD BEEN WITH JESUS

When they saw the courage of Peter and John and realized that they were unschooled, ordinary men, they were astonished and they took note that these men had been with Jesus. (Acts 4:13)

I received Jesus into my heart at a Young Life meeting in Japan in the early 1970s. It was the height of the Jesus Movement that was sweeping the world. The only worship songs I had at the time were songs like Bob Dylan's "Blowin' in the Wind," a veiled reference to the Holy Spirit, and the Kurt Kaiser tune "Pass It On." It wasn't much, but songs like those were life to me, and I sat in my bedroom and played them for hours.

I remember those early days with Jesus in my bedroom. I felt a distinct sense of the presence of God. I remember it feeling so real that it seemed as if someone was in the room with me. It was the presence of Jesus. Do you remember those days?

After a few years, my family moved to California. My dad retired from the Marines and ended up working at Camp Pendleton. I started working at a brand-new Christian bookstore in Vista, California. The owners discovered I played the guitar, gave me two praise books, told me to learn the songs, and asked me to play for their Bible study.

Excited to do something new and fresh, I learned the songs and went to the Bible study. They asked me to "lead worship." I didn't know what that was, so I simply closed my eyes and sang. When I did, I sensed the presence of Jesus as I did when I played in my bedroom. When I opened my eyes, I looked around the room and saw faces aglow, tears streaming down cheeks, hands lifted up.

I had no formal training as a worship leader. No one told me how to put a set list together. I just did in public what I did in private with Jesus. When things get too complicated, too technical, too production centered . . . I just remember those early days with Jesus.

If you've forgotten what it was like to simply be with Jesus, may I encourage you to go back? Remember what it was like and reinvent those moments in your present tense. In other words, return to your first love. What you'll find is that Jesus will be there waiting to meet with you, arms open wide.

Today's Prayer

Lord, help me remember that it's not my skill, my talent, my amazing tone, or my ministry that you love, but it's me that you love. I don't want anything to get in the middle of spending time with you. Let others see your presence in and around me. Amen.

Holland Davis
Pastor
Worship Life Calvary Chapel
San Clemente, California

24 ········• A WINNING POSITION

> So Christ himself gave the apostles, the prophets, the evangelists, the pastors and teachers, to equip his people for works of service, so that the body of Christ may be built up until we all reach unity in the faith and in the knowledge of the Son of God and become mature, attaining to the whole measure of the fullness of Christ.
> *(Ephesians 4:11-13)*

September 11, 1955, was a magical day for my dad, Del Crandall. He was the starting catcher for the Milwaukee Braves. On that Sunday afternoon the Philadelphia Phillies were in town to play at Milwaukee County Stadium. It was a hard-fought game, and in the bottom of the ninth the Braves found themselves down four to one. They had to get themselves into a position to win. The Braves loaded the bases and, with two outs, the twenty-five-year-old catcher from Southern California came up to bat. This is the scene that has been played out in the imagination of every kid who ever played Little League baseball. The count was three balls and two strikes, with two outs. The Braves had put themselves in a position to win this game, now it was all up to the hitter. After fouling off two more pitches from Phillies pitcher Herm Wehmeier, my dad hit a grand slam, scoring four runs to win the game. At that time, he was only the twelfth player in baseball history to hit a walk-off grand slam. That is quite an accomplishment, but it couldn't have happened unless his teammates had done their part to put the Braves into a position to win and my dad had prepared as a hitter for that moment. One player cannot win a baseball game.

The church is similar in that we all have our roles to play. Church leadership is there to prepare the church to do the work of the gospel. As a worship leader, I have always thought that it is my job to train the worship team, spiritually and musically, to ready the church for God's Word. For the church to grow in faith and knowledge of Christ and to mature in Him, it must be receptive to the teaching of the Scriptures. The dilemma is that if we don't prepare to lead worship, we become a distraction.

Are you preparing for the work of the gospel? Are you ready both spiritually and musically to lead worship? When you think about it, every time we lead worship, the situation before us is a potential game winner. Leading worship is one of the most important parts of any church service. We must be ready to hit it out of the park. After all, this is God whom we are worshiping.

Today's Prayer

Lord, thank you for the opportunity you have given me to serve you. I don't want to take it for granted, but instead I want to cherish every moment. Today, I commit to time in the Bible and prayer in order to prepare myself spiritually to lead worship. I also commit to preparing myself musically to lead God's people in worship. Amen.

Jeff Crandall
Worship Pastor
High Desert Church
Victorville, California

25 ·······• THE JOY OF THORNS

> To keep me from becoming conceited, I was given a thorn in my flesh .
> . . to torment me. Three times I pleaded with the Lord to take it away
> from me. But he said to me, "My grace is sufficient for you, for my
> power is made perfect in weakness." *(2 Corinthians 12:7-9)*

When I imagine a thorn, my thoughts fade from the beauty of a rose. Unharmonious is its sweet fragrance with that piercing sting, its delicate petals with such jagged edges. Yet even more illogical it would seem that the Lord reconciles my disarray by His perfect grace. I can hardly fathom that God loves me enough to puncture my heart with *His* thorn, opening the blockages with *His* blood, ultimately healing my wounds by *His* very own nail-scarred hands.

George Matheson was a Scottish pastor who became blind at the age of twenty. Abandoned by his fiancée, his intense heartbreak prompted him to pen the words to the great hymn "O Love That Wilt Not Let Me Go." On the eve of his sister's wedding he wrote:

> *O Joy that seekest me thro' pain,*
> *I cannot close my heart to Thee.*
> *I trace the rainbow thro' the rain,*
> *And feel the promise is not vain*
> *That morn shall tearless be.*

Only by *trusting* wholly in Christ does so deep a thorn produce so lasting a joy, bearing fruit that outlives generations.

Joni Eareckson Tada is another person whose thorn has touched the lives of many who have suffered. She became a quadriplegic in a diving accident as a teenager, but through perseverance in Jesus she has triumphed to emerge as a successful author, artist, and speaker. Now in her sixth decade, she is bravely facing a cancer that threatens her very existence. Still, she continues to praise God with gladness of heart, saying, "I want to assure you that I am genuinely content to receive from God whatever He deems fit for me."

Only by *faith* in the risen Christ does so devastating a thorn yield so fulfilling a purpose.

My nephew, Zachary, was paralyzed at the tender age of ten. For six years now he has been my personal example of relentless joy in spite of the thorn. Unbeknownst to her, when my sister named him Zachary Storm, she was foreshadowing his life's tumultuous journey that has included seizures, multiple medical challenges, and then the loss of his mobility. Yet there has never been a moment when I can't remember "Zach Attack" with a smile . . . and oh, that infectious laugh! He lives life with a fierce determination to bring happiness to all circumstances. I remember my sister recalling once when Zach was in time-out alone in his room singing one of my songs, "Free, I'm free! Jesus granted clemency!"

Only with hope from his Abba Father does a child view such a debilitating thorn as the window to freedom.

To be candid, though, I wish the Lord had created roses without thorns. The "me of little faith" hopes I never have to experience blindness, cancer, or being confined to a wheelchair. And if I'm really honest, there are still times when I fear the valley of the shadow of death. But through it all, I know my God will most certainly be there, right alongside the thorns . . . *my* Rose of Sharon, filling me with joy in His presence.

Today's Prayer

"My God, I have never thanked Thee for my 'thorn!' I have thanked Thee a thousand times for my roses, but never once for my 'thorn;' I have been looking forward to a world where I shall get compensation for my cross as itself a present glory. Teach me the glory of my cross; teach me the value of my 'thorn.' Show me that I have climbed to Thee by the path of pain. Show me that my tears have made my rainbow." (George Matheson).

Stefanie Kelly
Worship Arts Pastor
Rock Church
San Diego, California

26 ·······• PUT YOUR PRAISE ON

> The Spirit of the Sovereign LORD is on me, because the LORD has anointed me . . . to comfort all who mourn, and provide for those who grieve in Zion—to bestow on them a crown of beauty instead of ashes, the oil of joy instead of mourning, and a garment of praise instead of a spirit of despair. *(Isaiah 61:1-3)*

Looking back at my ministry over the past twenty-five years, I see God has placed me in churches that have had corporate hurt and unfortunate circumstances in their histories. I came into these churches at a time when healing and special ministry was needed. I didn't choose this type of ministry, but for whatever reason, God placed me in these circumstances. I have learned through this that God uses our praise to bring healing. God is the one who does the changing, but He will also use those who choose to worship Him and praise Him through trials to bring encouragement and change in others, even the congregation as a whole. What is true for the individual is true for the congregation.

God did this work in my life. In the fall of 1998 I was suddenly and surprisingly diagnosed with a brain tumor. Today I still live with this medical condition and continue to serve as a worship pastor. I consider this tumor a gift from God because it has taught me to better praise Him and worship Him. Through this experience, I was faced with a choice: *will I praise Him or will I become bitter?* By the grace of God, I chose to give Him praise. That choice not only brought a needed positive impact on my life, but God used it to bring a positive change in those I led each week. As the scripture reminds us, He brought a "garment of praise instead of a spirit of despair." My circumstances won't change my praise, but my praise can change my circumstances.

This is true for the congregation. When the church gathers each week and there is a spirit of praise, worship, celebration, and joy in our worship music, it permeates the church so that the spirit of praise replaces the spirit of heaviness or despair. It's contagious.

So, my challenge to the congregation is to make the choice to "Put your praise on!" You don't have to live with the spirit of mourning and despair. You were created to praise!

Today's Prayer

Lord, by your grace I choose praise. No matter the trials that come my way, I want to honor you and encourage others with my praise. I pray that I will have a thankful heart and be free from bitterness. I choose praise. Amen.

Joel Allen
Worship Arts Pastor
Immanuel Baptist Church
Wichita, Kansas

27 ········• TOWERING FAITH

Be strong and courageous. Do not be afraid or terrified because of them, for the LORD your God goes with you; he will never leave you nor forsake you. *(Deuteronomy 31:6)*

A few years ago, my husband, Joel, our two oldest children, and I attended a conference in Las Vegas. For most tourists one of the points of interest in Las Vegas is going to the Stratosphere Tower, which is 1,149 feet (350 m) high, making it the tallest free-standing observation tower in the United States.

Because I am afraid of heights, I diligently tried to offer other suggestions to my family. I suggested the local water park, or Circus Circus, and many other safer forms of entertainment (all of which are on level ground). After much discussion we were on our way to the Stratosphere (obviously my power of persuasion needed some punch).

As we stood in line for the elevator, I wondered what in the world I had gotten myself into. I began to go through a gamut of emotions. I was sweating. Sick to my stomach. Nervous. Scared. Dizzy. Just then the elevator door opened and there was no escaping. Up we went.

When we arrived at the top we cautiously exited the elevator. Suddenly I froze in my tracks. Right in front of us was a 360-degree view of nothing but straight down. My knees were knocking so hard I thought I was shaking the tower, but actually the wind was howling so hard that day that the entire structure was swaying. Oh what fun.

I remembered praying, *God, please don't let anyone touch me. Don't let there be an earthquake. Please keep the elevators working. And let me get out of this crazy thing!*

It was there at the top of a tower in Las Vegas that I gained a whole new revelation of faith. I was totally out of control. I could not change a thing, and I could not leave until the next elevator arrived.

Ever felt like this? Scared, uncertain, and nervous . . . but it seems that you can't change a thing?

Life has a way of putting you in situations in which it seems you have no control and you're all alone. But no matter what you're facing, God is always with you, holding you up, giving you comfort, and protecting you.

When you do get down from your tower you'll realize that it allowed your faith to grow . . . and maybe even gave you a little fun in the process.

Today's Prayer

Jesus, I thank you that you know all about me and that you love me. Sometimes I'm scared, and I don't know what to do. Your Word says I don't need to worry about today or tomorrow. Help me put my faith in you more today than I did yesterday, knowing that you will take care of every detail concerning me. You're an awesome God, and I love you. Amen.

Kathie Phillips
Director of Worship and Arts
Escondido Christian Center
Escondido, California

28 ....• A RAINBOW IN THE CLOUDS

Whenever the rainbow appears in the clouds, I will see it and remember the everlasting covenant between God and all living creatures of every kind on the earth. *(Genesis 9:16)*

A few years ago, some of my closest friends turned out to be my worst enemies. They betrayed my trust, talked about me behind my back, and lied to my face. There were times during the demise of these relationships that I actually felt that they were part friend and part enemy. My love for them ran deep. Our relationship spanned a decade. I did everything I could to work things out, but after it was all said and done we parted ways, albeit with kind words. I was hurt, confused, and felt as though a cloud had made its habitation directly over my heart.

Through this experience I learned betrayal can be extremely damaging to a person's sense of security and reality. It makes you question your judgment about everything in life. As a worship leader, the disconnect with my friends put a damper even on my ability to deeply connect with the Father during worship. Yet as I prayed about all of this, the still, small voice of the Holy Spirit consistently impressed on me that I did not need to chase some kind of resolution because the separation was needed, timely, and would turn out for my best in the end. These words were incredibly comforting, and they became a rainbow in the clouds for me.

Everybody loves a rainbow. Seeing one often brings about feelings of awe, wonder, and hope. Rainbows are breathtaking. But isn't it ironic that rainbows usually come after storms? These dazzling, beauty-filled symbols of God's covenant and presence reveal themselves after gray, depressing clouds and rain have ruined our plans and made life momentarily miserable. Then, slowly, the sun begins to shine. The clouds part, and the rainbows magically appear just long enough to redirect our vision.

This is when we need rainbows most—in the midst of the clouds. We need to see those gigantic, multicolored arches staring down on us as the clouds of life roll away. There they stand. Proud and tall as if they were just waiting for us to look up and be inspired by them. There they hover—reminding us that God is merciful and that there is still plenty of security and hope left after the storm.

I wonder if the rainbow helped Noah worship this God who had allowed destruction to take over the world. I think it most likely did. After the flood, Noah probably shuddered every time a few drops of rain began to fall. But then he pulled himself together when that big bow in the sky stood up. Maybe he even chased a few rainbows just to see if he could better capture God's covenant promise to always provide security—in spite of disappointment.

Today's Prayer

Father, the signs of your commitment to me are all around. May I not look to the things that are temporal to find my refuge, but may I look to you and you alone. Cause my worship to be as eternal as your promises are to me. Amen.

Marlinda Ireland
Worship Leader
Christ Church
Montclair, New Jersey

29 ····• TAKING A SECOND LOOK AT PRAISE

> But may the righteous be glad and rejoice before God; may they be happy and joyful. Sing to God, sing in praise of his name, extol him who rides on the clouds; rejoice before him—his name is the LORD. A father to the fatherless, a defender of widows, is God in his holy dwelling. *(Psalm 68:3-5)*

A few years into serving as a worship pastor at a large church in San Diego, I met Dennis Sempebwa of Limit X, a music group from Uganda. Their music has been described as "a wonderfully turbulent rhythmic brew of elements of United States dance floor funk mixed with African street rhythms." When Limit X ministered at our church, an amazing congregational transformation took place. There was a new level of joy. There was freedom. There was, yes, even dancing!

Dennis and Limit X came from Uganda to the church in America as musical missionaries (musicianaries). They came to strengthen and encourage the church to grow in their expression of praise to God. Dennis described their times of praise and worship in Uganda as "holy chaos," much like you'd find at a sporting event in the United States. "We'd walk miles to church through unimaginable peril and danger," Dennis said. "In spite of our poverty and lack, we praised God, not because of what He'd done for us, but because of who He *is!* Every moment in His presence was precious because we did not know if we'd have another opportunity." They sang and danced before the Lord for hours. Without pulpit direction, the Holy Spirit ministered in this environment of praise, healing, and delivering many.

Dennis once told me of the faith of a young mother who had lost her baby. She brought the lifeless body to church the following morning, concealed under her clothes. As thousands praised God, His power raised the baby back to life!

Dennis said, "In Africa, we have kings. Real kings have absolute authority. You don't get to choose what rules to obey. If you get an audience with a king, in preparation, you learn about his accolades, conquests, and so on. Once through the palace gates, you literally begin to shout his praises: 'Who is like this great king? He has vanquished lands and protected his people. What a mighty king we have!' Everyone makes room for you, because they know you are on your way to see the king. People know that if you get an audience with the king, he has the power and authority to grant you anything he wants. In the United States you elect your leaders, and if you don't like their policies, you vote them out. You are constantly evaluating whether or not you agree with leadership and whether to submit to them. Christianity is *kingdom*. We serve an absolute God. The Bible is not a menu. We are His subjects, and it's for His pleasure that we live. It's very hard for Americans, who live in a democracy, to embrace this kingdom mind-set."

In a time when we often refer to the upbeat, faster tempo songs as *praise* and the power ballads as *worship*, I am encouraged to reexamine the Scriptures and see what my King has to say about praise. If lifting up His name falls under the category of praise, consider this: invest more time *praising* God together and *lifting* up His name higher and higher because of who He is and what He has done. I believe this will have a direct impact on the depth of our worship time together.

Today's Prayer

Lord, develop in me a heart that longs to bring you glory, that desires to honor your name with everything I am, that prefers to bless your name above what anyone around me might think of me. You are a Mighty King, and I have come to praise you for who you are and what you have done! Amen.

Roy Cochran
Worship Pastor and Pastor to Artists
Worship Mentor Network
Carlsbad, California

30 ·······• THE GRAND REVERSAL

> "Quick! Bring the best robe and put it on him. Put a ring on his finger and sandals on his feet. Bring the fattened calf and kill it. Let's have a feast and celebrate. For this son of mine was dead and is alive again; he was lost and is found." So they began to celebrate.
> *(Luke 15:22-24)*

A few years ago, someone I had once been very close to came back into my life. I dreaded seeing him and, frankly, put it off as long as I could. For years I'd played the victim, dragging my wounds and anger behind me like some banged-up, rusty trunk. Remember the priest played by Robert DeNiro in the film *The Mission*? He strapped all of his material possessions to his back, symbolizing all the sins he'd committed for which he believed there was no forgiveness.

I was like that priest. Except it wasn't my own sin and guilt I was carrying, but an endless, self-righteous tally of wrongs others—especially this person—had done to me. For years I lacked momentum and peace in my life and wondered why. But the answer had been there all the time. Resentment and bitterness were draining me of life.

When our meeting finally came, it was in the visitation room of a prison. But this was not an inquisition. It was a celebration. Six hours of pure grace. The "accused" opened his arms in greeting, just as the prodigal son's father had done, letting go a hearty laugh the moment he saw me—laughter that lifted my heart as nothing else has done in my entire life. Laughter that meant all was well. And it truly was.

How ironic. My prodigal heart had been met and embraced by the one I had labeled the prodigal. But in this grand reversal, I received a gift of untold value—a gift that changed my life. In those six hours, God gave me a mirror of unmitigated truth, and I saw myself more clearly than ever before. So much of my identity had been formed by building walls between myself and others. So much of my energy had been drained as I white-knuckled my grip on pain. No question about it, my inability to let go reflected deep flaws. But there in the mirror was another truth shining back at me: I am also a child of God, more deeply loved than I am flawed.

Jesus came to show us there is a different way. We can receive grace freely and give it just as freely. We can become servants of love instead of hostility. Like the father who ran toward his wayward son, we can break the cycle of self-righteousness, hurt, anger, and enmity—as individuals, as communities, and as nations.

Today's Prayer

> *Lord, may we seek to embrace others as you have embraced us—*
> *without judgment, without condition. Amen.*

Sally Morgenthaler
Founder, Breakthrough Coaching
(Practical Help for Churches Who Want to Make a Difference)
Centennial, Colorado

31 ·········• SWEETLY BROKEN

Do not let your hearts be troubled. You believe in God; believe also in me. *(John 14:1)*

Fear is a miserable companion. It begins in the pit of my stomach before my mind even registers its existence. It cloaks itself in depression and sometimes anger. It insinuates itself into every response, masking its true position as an idol in my heart with euphemisms like *worry* and *concern*. The reality is that I have some major trust issues. The fact that I'm an oldest child should not justify my unwillingness to relinquish control, but it's an excuse I often spout with just enough of a smile that I seem transparent and able to laugh at my own foibles.

One evening, our worship pastor, Ryan, slipped a song into the set that we hadn't rehearsed. It was the hymn—updated and accompanied by electric guitar, of course—"I Surrender All." *Ummm. Yeah. Can we just skip that one?*

Here's the thing. I don't want to. Surrender all, that is. It's too frightening for me, especially when what I see looks hopeless. I find myself focusing on the difficult situations around me. My fears start to compound, and I am unable to see God working in any of it.

I should make it quite clear that I have witnessed God's grace. I have received His mercy and blessing more times than I can recount. I *know* God has carried me through some debilitating times with a clarity that I wish I could hold onto for more than a brief moment.

So, returning to our unplanned worship set, we came out of communion singing "I Surrender All," and I was fighting it. My attempts to disengage started to erode somewhere around verse two:

> *All to Jesus I surrender;*
> *Humbly at His feet I bow,*
> *Worldly pleasures all forsaken.*
> *Take me, Jesus, take me now.*

Slowly the layers of resolve began to peel away despite my best efforts to stay ticked off at God. The set was orchestrated to move from "I Surrender All" into "Sweetly Broken" by Jeremy Riddle, with me leading. By the time I hit the chorus I had to drop out. I broke. The tears streamed down my face as I was reminded anew that God is love, and God is just.

I was so beautifully brought into recognition of His sovereignty despite my willful distrust. Now on the mornings when the pit in my stomach takes up its normal residency, I pray Christ will invade my space moment by moment in that day. That He will reveal himself to me in ways that assault my selfish nature and infringe on my comfort. That He will continue to humble me and transform my yearnings until they align with His will. That His kingdom will come, His will be done in my heart and life as it is in heaven.

Today's Prayer

Lord, break my will today to conform to yours. I want to focus on you, not on what causes me to fear. Remind me of your sovereignty as I seek to make you known. Amen.

Melissa Baldwin
Worship Leader/Songwriter
Crossroads Church
National City, California

32 ·······• WORSHIPING WARRIORS

Through the praise of children and infants you have established a
stronghold against your enemies, to silence the foe and the avenger.
(Psalm 8:2)

Several years ago I had the privilege of helping lead a King's Kids International ministry team on a tour of Europe. This particular team was a delightful mosaic of youngsters from thirteen different countries, ages five to eighteen, with a mission to "declare the glory of God among the nations" through the venue of the performing arts. Utilizing dynamic multimedia, international costumes, energetic music, and dance, these young ambassadors of joy captured the imaginations of audiences all across Europe.

One cool, beautiful evening right on the streets of downtown West Berlin, the young people had drawn a huge crowd with their production. The audience was engaged and very responsive, enjoying the presentation immensely. At the climax of the program the young people sang a medley of worship songs in preparation to tell their stories and for the gospel to be shared. While they were worshiping, a large group of militant punk rockers began doing lewd dances around the stage and taunting the kids. Those of us in leadership became concerned about the intentions of the intruders because, at that time, there had been many outbreaks of violence at gatherings of punk rockers in Europe. We began to pray.

As the music began to swell, the young people's focus on God intensified, and they were oblivious to all that was going on around them. The atmosphere was electric, and the powerful presence of God in the midst of this pure presentation of praise and worship from these children exposed the darkness motivating the songs and dances of the punk rockers. The crowd simply silenced the punk rockers and told them to leave or be quiet. The young people finished their worship medley, and a powerful presentation of the gospel followed. The Lord literally ordained (used) praise from the mouths of children to silence the foe and the avenger.

Over the years, as I have encountered dark moments of spiritual oppression and attack, I have remembered this incredible picture of the purity and power of simple, childlike praise and worship. It has encouraged me to declare the character and glory of the Lord with this same childlike faith in order to silence the foe and avenger and to beat back the forces of darkness coming against my life. These young people taught me that when darkness comes I need to focus on the Father instead of focusing on the darkness. It is much more effective.

Today's Prayer

Lord, when darkness comes my way help me focus the attention of my heart on you. Help me worship you with the sincerity and simplicity, the purity and the power, of childlike faith. Help me be a faithful, worshiping warrior. Amen.

Mike Harris
Founder and President
WaveMaker Ministries
Colorado Springs, Colorado

33 ······• STOP PERFORMING . . . START RELATING!

[Speak] to one another with psalms, hymns, and songs from the Spirit. Sing and make music from your heart to the Lord. *(Ephesians 5:19)*

M usic is all about building relationships with God and one another. This truth is easy to believe but sometimes difficult to apply. It's easy to get so busy serving God that we neglect our relationship with Him. If I asked you, "When was the last time God spoke to you?" what would you say? Our music is only as life-changing as our relationship with God (John 15:5). If our relationship with God is joyless, predictable, and distant, it's time to take the "Psalms challenge."

Each morning, ask God to reveal something new about himself that He wants you to know. Commit to reading a chapter a day in the Psalms. Keep reading the chapter over and over, underlining words and phrases that begin to stand out to you. Eventually God will reveal himself or something He wants you to know. When He does—and this is the most important step—be sure to journal your prayer, thanking God for what He revealed to you, and then date it. It will become a daily, physical marker of each intimate spiritual encounter you have with God.

Now you are ready to "make music from your heart to the Lord."

Once your heart is right, it's time to give God a great offering by practicing, owning, and making song lyrics a real conversation between you and God (Colossians 3:23). When you do, don't forget to invite the church to join in on your conversation with God. This is the "speaking to one another" part in Ephesians 5.

Relationships happen one life at a time. The harvest field is not the crowd, but individuals in the crowd. It's easy to scan audiences, but it requires an authentic leader to look into the individual eyes of the people. It keeps you real.

Don't forget the people on the platform who are serving with you. When someone plays or sings a note that freshly paints the worship picture, turn and immediately mark that moment with a smile or a head nod (Hebrews 10:24). It's important for the congregation to see authentic love relationships between musicians on the stage (John 13:35).

Don't get so hung up on the music that you sacrifice relationship for performance. Certainly give God a great offering by practicing in advance and giving your best (Psalm 33:3). But remember it is not perfection but *excellence,* which is doing the best you can, that honors God and inspires people.

A few years ago, a lady stopped me after a service. She said, "I always thought God was like my earthly father: stern, unloving, and displeased. When you were leading worship, you looked at me and smiled. In that moment, I experienced God smiling through you and loving me for the first time in my life!"

People will remember your relationship with them long after they forget your songs. She couldn't remember the song, but she remembered the smile.

Ask God to help you start building better relationships through His music. It will change your life and the lives of others.

Today's Prayer

Lord, forgive me for performing music without authentic relationship. Jesus, help me lead music that builds relationships with you and your people. Help me reflect you in a way that makes an eternal difference. Amen.

Paul Black
Music and Worship Pasator
NorthRidge Church
Plymouth, Michigan

34 ········• TOO GOOD TO BE TRUE AND SO MUCH MORE

Keep me safe, my God, for in you I take refuge. I said to the Lord, "You are my Lord; apart from you I have no good thing." *(Psalm 16:1-2)*

This seemed like an easy scripture to memorize. I knew after reading it that I wanted to have it fashioned in my soul. I was frustrated at how long it took to memorize what seemed like a fairly simple scripture. However, I kept reading it over and over again until I had it.

Months later I entered a difficult season. I wrestled with health challenges that caused me to wonder if I could still praise God with a worshipful heart if He took away control of my voice and hands. Then after years of my wife and me trying to have a baby, we had two separate adoption situations open up to us at the same time. We weren't yet seeking out adoption, but it seemed like God was in it. In a matter of 120 days, however, both birth moms changed their minds, and we were crushed. All this was going on while I felt God leading me to start a new commission-only job right when the economy crashed. We went six months without a paycheck. God used that time to carve places in my heart He could not have formed any other way.

I held on to Psalm 16:1-2 and prayed it often. I prayed for God's safety to protect me physically, financially, and emotionally. I remember dropping to my knees, weeping out loud. I cried as it hurt emotionally to trust Him, but I had nowhere else to turn. So I tried with everything I had to love God through the pain.

I considered turning my back on God. I knew He was real, but I thought if I chose not to serve Him perhaps I wouldn't get my hopes up and run into disappointment. On Easter Sunday that year I remember singing the same worship songs repeatedly in rehearsal and multiple services. As I continued to consciously choose Jesus, He began to lift the heaviness from me. I found in those moments all I could do was continually offer myself to Him and say with my heart, "You are my Lord; apart from you I have no good thing."

As God began to transform my heart, He brought amazing blessing and healing physically, financially, and emotionally. On May 28, 2009, we received a call from the local adoption agency. There was a two-day-old baby girl in need of a family immediately. We rushed to buy a car seat and came home that night with a daughter. Exactly twelve months later God showed His greatness again by bringing us an amazing son with very short notice. Our children wouldn't have found us without going through the journey God led us through. We read stories in the Bible of God's goodness, but it's even greater when He demonstrates in a personal way that apart from His grace we have no good thing.

Today's Prayer

God, you are so good and so much more than we could ever hope for. Help us take refuge in you, and help us remember when we go through the valley that apart from you we have no good thing. Amen.

Rocky Barra
Worship Leader
<www.slingshotgroup.net>
Orlando, California

35 ········• WORSHIPER

> Search me, God, and know my heart; test me and know my anxious
> thoughts. See if there is any offensive way in me, and lead me in the
> way everlasting. *(Psalm 139:23-24)*

After leading worship every weekend for more than twenty
years, I recently went through a new experience and change
in my understanding of worship. No longer leading every service, I
became a participant, a member of the body, no longer onstage or
producing music or the culture of worship.

At first, the freedom to just attend and not be responsible for
anything was euphoric.

For the first time in my marriage I was able to go to church and
sit with my wife. No set lists to prepare, no rehearsals, no sound
checks, no pressure. I could just come to the service and leave
at the end. No meetings during the week to digest and plan. I . . .
was . . . free.

As the new season in my life continued, though, I became agitated and felt lost. I no longer knew who I was because I was no longer doing the things I'd done and known for years. Worship services that had been life-giving had now become painful, and I was no longer free. Instead of a worshiper, I had become a spectator—like those people I used to see at the back of the sanctuary with their arms crossed. I lost my voice to sing in total freedom and abandonment before my King. Instead, I struggled to engage and press in.

Was it jealousy? No, I'd always encouraged new leaders and musicians to grow in their gifts, preferring others to step into the spotlight. Was it ambition? No, I had been and done everything God had put on my heart to do. I was just genuinely lost, not knowing my place or who I was anymore.

As I struggled, God revealed that my identity had become wrapped up in leading worship. If I wasn't leading or playing my guitar or singing, I didn't know who I was! When I led occasionally, I sensed an incredible freedom and anointing. Like riding a bike, it all came back. But God wanted to show me a new season and a new identity, not defined by my gifts or reputation or history—one defined only by Him. It was time for me to learn to worship the true I AM, not who I am . . . or thought I was.

As I looked around at my spiritual mentors and listened to their stories, I realized we go through seasons; our roles change, but our gifts and calling don't. We shepherd and lead wherever we are. My worship has become directed by the Word, not by a sermon series or upcoming service. My face is planted on the ground before God alone, thanking Him for who He is and for the unmerited favor and grace shown to me.

Today's Prayer

Lord, search me, test me, and remove any idol, thought, or pattern that has kept me from worshiping you. I want to follow your leading. Forgive me for getting it mixed up. Amen.

Stan Sinclair
Worshiper
Reality Church
Carpinteria, California

36 ·······• A SIMPLE ACT OF OBEDIENCE

> But Samuel replied: "Does the Lord delight in burnt offerings and sacrifices as much as in obeying the voice of the Lord? To obey is better than sacrifice, and to heed is better than the fat of rams."
> *(1 Samuel 15:22)*

I would not be a worship leader today if I had said no.

My wife, C.C., and I were two of the forty-five hundred people worshiping together that night.

The title of the song was "I Lift Up My Hands."

Israel Houghton was leading infectiously! As I glanced around, it seemed like every single person in that auditorium had his or her hands up in the air.

But I felt as though there was a spotlight on me.

My thoughts jumbled together.

What's wrong with me? Everyone in this place is lifting up their hands. Why are my shoulders so heavy?

God, I love you, I prayed. *I love to worship you. I'm moved in this moment to honor you because of your greatness and your love. So why are my hands glued to my sides?*

The "voice" began to speak.

"Lift your hands."

I can't. You know my heart. Why do I have to do something that's uncomfortable for me? You know I grew up Baptist! (Okay, I didn't actually think in those exact terms.)

"I want to take you beyond what you've known before. You can trust me."

Looking back, the moment had very little to do with God somehow being more honored when our hands are closer to Him. I have to think that a good percentage of the packed house wasn't actually any closer to God because they had their hands in the air and their eyes closed.

But it had everything to do with whether I was going to respond in obedience, to let go of control and risk giving myself over to Him.

There was no doubt that the Spirit of God was close, and He was asking me to physically remove my hands from my pockets and raise them vertically. We were in a tug of war, and as strange as it sounds, I was stronger. I could've continued to worship in my own way and left that night feeling moved, having had an experience with God that deepened my belief in Him.

But I would have missed out on so much more.

After a brief pit stop with my elbows still at my sides, palms up, I just went for it. I closed my eyes and thrust my hands upward, shaking.

I put my head down because I felt so exposed.

But in that moment, something broke loose inside me, and the tears started flowing.

As silly as this situation seems, especially as I type it out for faceless strangers, there was so much at stake.

The struggle and the eventual victory of obedience changed me. I learned to place value on small acts of obedience. God is honored—not as much by the show but by my willingness to hear His voice and respond with a yes.

I believe that a bunch of small yeses add up to experiencing the character of Christ fully formed in me.

Today's Prayer

Jesus, what is the one small step you are asking me to take? The one courageous decision you want me to risk? Obedience is not a once-and-done thing. I want to continue to worship you by saying yes today. Speak to me and give me the courage to respond. Amen.

Stephen Claybrook
Worship Pastor
Crosspointe Church
Cary, North Carolina

37 ········• FOR FUTURE PLAYBACK

Let this be recorded for future generations, so that a people not yet born will praise the LORD. Tell them the LORD looked down from his heavenly sanctuary. He looked down to earth from heaven to hear the groans of the prisoners, to release those condemned to die. And so the LORD's fame will be celebrated in Zion, his praises in Jerusalem, when multitudes gather together and kingdoms come to worship the LORD. *(Psalm 102:18-22 NLT)*

I returned home late from a preproduction rehearsal and got only a few hours of sleep. Before I returned to the studio the next morning, my wife, Brittany, read Psalm 102:18-22.

The word *recorded* in the first line jumped off the page at me because I was on the verge of entering the studio to record a few songs. I dove further in; I could taste the hope in the moment. This was no simple instruction for us to write something down or take note of what was being said. It was a promise unfolding in the present. It was a challenge for me to live each moment knowing it was recorded for future playback.

Do I live a life that may sing for future generations?

As a worship leader and songwriter, sometimes it's hard to avoid only playing that new hit song or writing easy, surface lyrics. After reading that passage, though, I began thinking about the importance of the songs I was to record. Based on my understanding of this scripture and the connection it made in my spirit, I was determined to see the hope for future generations fused into my practical recording process.

My eyes remain open to this scripture. I ponder the weight of its meaning in my life. It has become much more than a theme to a song or an album.

When meditating on those words, I envisioned joining people and walking through the desert with great excitement toward a river ahead. We knew this river—we freely came and went from it. It was clear to me this river was symbolizing the Spirit of God. Along the way we began passing by many hurting people: blind, suicidal, divorced, impoverished, crippled, orphaned, disease-stricken, hungry, and thirsty. They were just lying there condemned to die. Away we went—only slowing, to step over the hopeless. I was in the middle; I could see that some had reached the river and some were approaching its banks. At that moment, everything inside of me knew the river was not for us alone. Our time was recorded. We were purposed to pick up the feeble unlovables and carry them to the deep waters of hope.

Today's Prayer

Lord, your waters are deeper than I could ever explore alone. May I live a life that is recorded as your promise for generations to come—a life that lifts the cripple into your stirring waters, brings the thirsty into your living springs, and splashes with the broken in oceans of hope so that we may all gather and praise you in Zion. Amen.

D. Taylor Maxwell
Worship Leader
YWAM Orlando, Florida
Orlando North Community Church
Orlando, Florida

38 ········• WE'RE ALL ADOPTED

For he chose us in him before the creation of the world to be holy
and blameless in his sight. In love he predestined us for adoption to
sonship through Jesus Christ, in accordance with his pleasure and
will—to the praise of his glorious grace, which he has freely given
us in the One he loves. In him we have redemption through his blood,
the forgiveness of sins, in accordance with the riches of God's grace
that he lavished on us. With all wisdom and understanding, he made
known to us the mystery of his will. *(Ephesians 1:4-8)*

We all have a story. I try to remember this each week as I lead
worship: to not just see people, but their stories as well. The
greatest gift we can give as lead worshipers is to somehow connect
people and their stories with God's story, because that's where we
find true value, meaning, and purpose.

Recently our local paper did an article on my family's story.
Apparently we were interesting enough to write about. I'm sure it
had something to do with me being from Australia, Mandy (my
wife) from England, and then our two boys from Chicago—now all

in Colorado. Also, we adopted our two boys at birth from the same birth mom exactly two years apart (really—born on the same day!). Our church was excited about the article, but one line that appeared in the final edit did not sit well with me at all. The line read: "The parenthood part of life wasn't easy to come by. The Foots have had to adopt their children." Have *had* to adopt their children? That made our boys sound like some kind of consolation prize.

Sure, infertility is part of our story. And so is adoption. But we didn't *have* to adopt our children. We wanted to! We felt called to. Even though our journey didn't go the way we planned, I wouldn't change a piece of it. When I look into the eyes of my boys, I better understand the heart of God. I know they were meant to be in our family from the beginning, and I love them with a love I've never known.

Likewise, adoption is part of your story. God didn't *have* to adopt us, He wanted to. We were meant to be in His family from the beginning, and He loves us with a love that He "lavished on us with all wisdom and understanding."

Through Christ we inherit the only story that can make sense of our lives, "to the praise of his glorious grace."

Today's Prayer

Father, thank you for adopting us as your children, for redeeming our stories, and for making sense of our lives and journeys. May you continue to write your story in and through us in accordance with your pleasure and will and for your eternal glory. Amen.

Tim Foot
Worship Pastor
LifeBridge Christian Church
Longmont, Colorado

39 ······• SPRINTING INTO SILENCE AND SOLITUDE

> God did this so that, by two unchangeable things in which it is impossible for God to lie, we who have fled to take hold of the hope set before us may be greatly encouraged. We have this hope as an anchor for the soul, firm and secure. It enters the inner sanctuary behind the curtain. *(Hebrews 6:18-19)*

In my first ten years in ministry, I poured my whole being into it. All my gifts, time, energy, and, yes, even my perfectionism. It did not take long before I began to feel tired, depleted, and even a bit depressed. I had hit a wall with a clear understanding that I was doing everything "just fine" but nothing "excellently." I felt shame and guilt, which led to anxiety and even a panic disorder as well. The bottom line was that I was at full-steam-ahead burnout.

I knew I needed help, so I decided to seek the assistance of a spiritual director. Her name was Sibyl. Sibyl lives with the knowledge that all of life is ministry. After some time and a lot of listening to me unpack my baggage, she concluded that I had given my best energies to the work of the ministry but not to the work of God in my life. I had been doing ministry in my own strength. Now my energy and passion were slowly leaving me.

She listened to the story that was my life and told me my pace was unsustainable and that "hurry" was my enemy. Sib said I needed to create a space for God to work and dwell. She then asked me if I had ever read anything by Henri Nouwen or ever practiced silence or solitude. My answer was, "Are you kidding? I vacuum while my TV and iPod are on." So Sibyl challenged me to spend some time with God alone, really alone. For once, no journal, no music, not even my Bible. Just sitting and being still with God. We decided three hours would be a good start. To be honest, though, I was a bit insulted with the lightweight timeframe. I thought surely I could do better than that. I drove to my local forest preserve and found a beautiful spot to reflect and listen. I prayed and prayed and thanked God for the beautiful nature around me. The time just flew by . . . or so I thought. To my surprise, when I looked at my watch only eight minutes had passed. I began to get frustrated by my lack of focus. Each time I began to pray I became distracted. I started thinking about my busy day and all the things I was behind on. I thought about my son's baseball game and if I needed to take goodies. I thought of all the friends I had not made contact with lately, and then the guilt seeped in. Overall, the time was a complete disaster. I felt like God was looking down on me and—rather than seeing a beloved daughter—He was seeing a weak, immature, spiritual wimp. I drove home after less than two hours thinking about what I would say to Sibyl when we met the next day. To be honest with you, I even considered telling her about what God laid on my heart during our "deeply rich time."

Pathetic!

The next morning I met with Sib, and the first thing I blurted out was, "I am a disaster! I can't even do three hours of silence. I was constantly distracted." When I shared with her my distractions, she gave me the best advice I have ever been given. "Andrea, pray into the distractions. When your mind goes to something, like Trent's baseball game, then see it as something from God and take it to Him."

Wow. What a concept!

So I began a journey (that means I am still in the process) of soul care when I get quiet with God one day a month. I start my time with these words, *God, I invite you into my mind, heart, and my day. Let me hear and see that everything is from you.* If a person pops into my head, I pray for him or her. If my son's ballgame pops into my head, I pray he will be an incredible example of Christ's love to his teammates and so on.

Today I am off the burnout path and leading my teams to do the same. Each month they take a day to get alone with God in quiet, and we hold one another accountable for it.

The outcome of this practice has changed my life and my ministry. My anxiety is significantly less. I almost never have panic episodes, and my ministry is paced and full of joy . . . at least most of the time.

"Solitude requires discipline; worship requires discipline; caring for others requires discipline. They all ask for us to set apart a time and a place where God's gracious presence can be acknowledged and responded to" (Henri Nouwen).

Today's Prayer

Father, help me remember that I am your beloved daughter whom you long to spend time with, to know, and to show love to. Help me create space for you to work and dwell in my life so my love for you will grow even stronger. Amen.

Andrea Minor
Executive Director, Chapel Arts Ministry
The Chapel
Libertyville, Illinois

40 ········• GOD USED A THORN

> Because of these surpassingly great revelations. . . . in order to keep me from being conceited, I was given a thorn in my flesh, a messenger of Satan, to torment me. Three times I pleaded with the Lord to take it away from me. But he said to me, "My grace is sufficient for you, for my power is made perfect in weakness." *(2 Corinthians 12:7-9)*

After being the worship leader at a fairly large church for four years, I developed a small problem. They're called hemorrhagic polyps, and the Vanderbilt Voice Center found two of them—one on each vocal fold. The problem is that the polyps kept me from singing, which is a bummer for a worship leader of any church, much less a large church.

I had surgery to remove the polyps, a process that took me out of leading worship for six months. One year after healing from the surgery and returning to worship leading, the polyps returned. So I had another surgery and another six months of not leading my church family in worship. And yes, it happened again. A year after the second surgery, the vocal polyps returned and I was forced to have yet another surgery and another six months away from doing what I love to do so much.

When I tally the total time away from worship leading, it was twenty months, which included a collective two months of total voice silence—quite a challenge for a sanguine. But it's quite amazing the things one hears when he or she can't talk. I listened like I had never listened before. I heard what people really said. Most important, I heard what God had to say. I believe God silenced me for that period to tell me a couple things.

God wanted me to learn that I was getting my significance from my job rather than my Jesus. That phrase is no cliché for me. It's real. After sitting in the congregation for twenty out of thirty-six months, God pointed out that I was too wrapped up in my status as a worship leader, that I was more proud of what I did rather than the One I was doing it for. Again, that is no cliché for me . . . it's real life.

While going through this learning experience, a friend of mine wrote me a short letter and asked this simple but penetrating question: "Greg, if God doesn't give you another gift except for the gift of grace in Jesus, will you be satisfied?" What my friend Marvin was really asking was whether or not I could worship if I could not sing. I hated that question, but God wanted me to face it.

The answer to that question came on a day when I had returned to leading worship after the third surgery. I could talk, but I wasn't supposed to sing yet. My pastor told me that I didn't need to sing to lead worship; I could simply lead the service, do the worship introductions, lead into the Lord's Supper, and pray. As for singing, he told me to just fake it—Milli Vanilli style. We chose two guys from the vocal team to rotate singing lead vocal for me. We did not tell the congregation. And it worked. But it worked too well. The first weekend I led worship without singing, a lady came to me after the service and said, "I hope you're not worried about your voice, you've never sounded better."

And so it goes. The thorn in my flesh was used by God to show me that it's not my ability, but His; it's not by my might, but by His Spirit. In my weakness, He is strong. It's not about me, it's about Him.

Today's Prayer

Father, thank you for speaking in the silence. May we be more acquainted with silence so that your voice is heard. Amen.

Greg Allen
Worship Pastor
Southeast Christian Church
Louisville, Kentucky

41 ········• KEEP THANKING ME

> Though the fig tree does not bud and there are no grapes on the vines, though the olive crop fails and the fields produce no food, though there are no sheep in the pen and no cattle in the stalls, yet I will rejoice in the Lord, I will be joyful in God my Savior. The Sovereign Lord is my strength; he makes my feet like the feet of a deer, he enables me to tread on the heights. *(Habakkuk 3:17-19)*

About ten years ago I was profoundly discouraged. I felt heaviness in my spirit that was almost tangible. We had a great home that had been on the market for a year and a half without one offer. We thought it would sell within six months, but we had not anticipated a severe economic downturn that almost froze home sales in their tracks. We were out of money with no good options left. I am not a depressed person, but the situation was so disheartening I could hardly speak.

I drove to an empty parking lot near where I lived and just sat there. The Lord spoke to me quietly, not in an audible way, but with a gentle nudging that I recognized as Him. I was so down I could not formulate the words to respond in prayer. The best I could do was a sort of "arghhhhh"—something between a choke and a sob. Softly, I sensed the Lord asking me to thank Him. With great difficulty, the words "thank you" congealed out of the dull fogginess in my mind.

The Lord prompted me to thank Him for something small. Like a little child learning to pray I obeyed haltingly, *Thank you for the sunshine.* Each word fought to escape my lips.

"Keep thanking me," I sensed the Lord say to my heart.

Thank you for that flower, I responded with a teeny bit more ease.

"I want you to be grateful," the Lord whispered to my innermost being. "I'm looking for you to have a heart filled with gratitude."

Gratitude engulfed me as I began to think of the many ways God had blessed my family and me. *Praise you, Lord, for how you met me here. Thank you for your kindness and your faithfulness. Thank you for what you are doing in my life and in my family. I trust you for your provision. Even if the circumstances are overwhelming, I choose to praise you and thank you. Thank you for the ability to choose to rejoice as I trust in your faithfulness.*

The heaviness lifted from me. I didn't know how things would resolve, but I drove home with a hopeful attitude. That night we received two offers on our home and completed the sale within thirty days.

My story might not have resolved that way. Habakkuk tells the story of a discouraged prophet. He knew the Assyrians were about to lay waste to Israel and lead God's people into captivity as slaves.

Yet Habakkuk chose to be grateful. Against unspeakable odds, he chose to rejoice.

"Keep thanking me," God said. I choose to do just that, one thank you at a time.

Today's Prayer

Lord, thank you for faithfully meeting with me. I trust you with every circumstance, and I will choose to praise you and rejoice in your presence. Amen.

Debbie Rettino
Director of Worship Leadership and Venues
Saddleback Church
Lake Forest, California

42 ·······• ETERNAL MOMENTS

> He has made everything beautiful in its time. He has also set eternity
> in the human heart; yet no one can fathom what God has done from
> beginning to end. *(Ecclesiastes 3:11)*

Death is a foreigner, a reality and fact of nature that I would rather live without. I thought I was prepared for my father's death two years ago. After several years of decline with Alzheimer's and Parkinson's, we all knew the day would be coming soon. But when the day arrived, I was no more prepared than if he had been perfectly healthy and died suddenly and unexpectedly. To watch a distinguished man of God, pastor for over fifty years, and loving father and husband slowly lose his identity and self brought more questions than answers to my grieving heart.

One meaningful answer came in the very last days of my father's time on earth. Having spent the evening with him, I watched as his caretaker prepared him for bed. After she got him all tucked in, she asked him, "Clyde, do you want to say your prayers?" By this time in his journey he was barely able to speak or even swallow. But his reply revealed to me the fully alive and thriving spirit in him: *Let the lost be found.* These were the words of his prayer. We could barely hear or understand him, so his caretaker asked him to repeat what he had said. "Let the lost be found," he said again. Five simple and profound words that still ring in my heart today.

My father never met a person he didn't share Christ with. Always the evangelist, he never let an opportunity pass him by. Here in his final days—his body almost gone, his mind already gone—his spirit still cried out for the lost to be found. At that moment, I knew Dad was still there. Still the strong leader I had always known him to be, even in his weakened state. Still united with the heart of Jesus, the One who left the ninety-nine to find the one lost sheep.

If God has put eternity in our hearts, no wonder death feels so foreign to us. We were not meant for it. We were meant for eternal communion with our Creator. And no wonder, also, that in worship we feel more at home than anywhere else. In worship we step into those eternal moments where the reality of life everlasting is most clear. In worship we join the chorus of angels and the saints who have gone before, where everything is beautiful forever.

Today's Prayer

Lord, thank you for eternal moments . . . moments where you give us glimpses into the unseen reality of your coming Kingdom. Thank you for humbling yourself, even to the point of death, so that we can live forever with you, the way you always wanted it to be. Amen.

Marsha Skidmore
Director of Contemporary Worship
First Presbyterian Church
Bakersfield, California

43 ········• WHAT'S YOUR NUMBER?

Do not store up for yourselves treasures on earth, where moths and vermin destroy, and where thieves break in and steal. But store up for yourselves treasures in heaven, where moths and vermin do not destroy, and where thieves do not break in and steal. For where your treasure is, there your heart will be also. *(Matthew 6:19-21)*

What's your number? We've all been asked that question for one reason or another. What's your phone number? What's your team jersey number? What's your guess for the jelly bean jar number? What's your class rank number?

Most recently, an investment company is asking that same question in their marketing campaign. They're asking what your dollar amount number is to bring you safety and comfort when you retire. "What is your number?" It seems humorous and harmless, but it says a lot about us as people. If a single number can define our safety or comfort or peace, what do we really value?

The scripture from Matthew talks about how we should approach our "number." It's a well-read passage from the Sermon on the Mount—the very words of Jesus himself. So we should pay attention to it, right? It seems like we should remember where our security lies, right? Not in earthly cash, mutual funds, or possessions, but rather in Christ, who offers a treasure in heaven that cannot be taken away. So simple, yet so difficult to pull off. So easy to read and agree with, yet so tough to put into practice. We often get sidetracked worrying about and placing so much importance on the gazillion dollars we need for security, when we should be living, breathing, and putting our hope in just *one* thing . . . Jesus.

So ask yourself again today, "What's my number?" Now pause. Read that passage again. Pause again. As a follower of Jesus, if your number is anything other than one, it's time to refocus and realign your life to the words of Jesus: "For where your treasure is, there your heart will be also."

Today's Prayer

Father, my security is in you. Let the worry and complications of life fall away as I put my hope in your treasures in heaven. Amen.

Matt Bayless
Worship Leader
Southeast Christian Church
Louisville, Kentucky

44 ·······• IS MY STYLE THE BEST?

Do nothing out of selfish ambition or vain conceit. Rather, in humility value others above yourselves, not looking to your own interests but each of you to the interests of the others. *(Philippians 2:3-4)*

W hen I arrived at a Christian college to teach a weeklong worship class, several students and faculty members told me about a young woman who was a fantastic singer/songwriter. When I finally heard her sing about three days into the class, I was equally impressed. She wasn't just singing notes and words, she was opening a door into her life that was vulnerable and refreshing. I knew she had a rare talent, and I was eager to encourage her to take her music and "get noticed."

I assumed she was regularly leading worship somewhere, doing concerts, and very much "in demand." However, as I talked with her I found she attended a small church of less than one hundred people in the swampy back roads of North Carolina. Even more shocking was that this beautiful young woman was asked only occasionally to sing in her home church. She seemed quite content to serve wherever she was needed—not insisting on a visible ministry in the church.

The style of worship in this little country church had not changed in forty years. Whoever led worship only needed to fill in the blanks of a worship order carved in stone. The older members of the church liked it that way, and this young woman was fine with that. She was okay flying just under the radar and had a genuine respect for those in the church who wanted things to stay the same.

As I got to know her more, I discovered her music of choice was the harder-edged music—considerably outside of the mainstream. It definitely would not be welcomed in her home church. It probably wouldn't even be found in the more progressive, youth-oriented churches in the country. And yet, because of her desire to put the interests of others before her own, she was willing to not only put up with the very different music of her church but actually see the positives in it.

What a challenge to me! As a worship leader, I have been guilty of pushing my own style onto others. Now, as I creep into my mid-forties, I find myself being the one trying to like the music of the younger generations. I also find my band members being critical of the musicality of those same young musicians. How did that happen? When did we become like our parents who reluctantly allowed long hair and drums into their church buildings in the 1970s?

Is it possible to live out Philippians 2 in the worship arena? What would it look like to submit to one another in worship? Maybe worship has more to do with offering something to God that is a beautiful representation of His varied creation instead of giving

Him something bland that doesn't involve sacrificing for others. Can worship be a rich celebration of our Creator where young and old, rich and poor, black and white not only tolerate the different ways we can sing of His fame but actually embrace them?

Today's Prayer

Lord, humble me. Your creation is so much bigger and more diverse than my little world and style preferences. Help me to show respect and honor to others—and to you—by appreciating the many ways you can be worshiped. Amen.

Phil Slocum
Worship Pastor
Central Christian Church
Lancaster, California

45 ········• THE OVERFLOW

May the God of hope fill you with all joy and peace as you trust in him, so that you may overflow with hope by the power of the Holy Spirit. (Romans 15:13)

It was early that Sunday morning when I was getting ready to leave for our service rehearsal. I saw my phone blinking with a text message, and I thought maybe one of our volunteers was sick or running late. Instead the message said, "Meagan didn't make it." I couldn't figure out what that meant. As I scrolled through the other texts, I quickly realized what was going on. I yelled out, "Oh no, God, please, no!" Rebecca, the wife of our friend and worship pastor, Leo Ahlstrom, and their twenty-four-year-old daughter, Meagan, had been hit by a drunk driver head-on, and Meagan didn't make it. I got to the hospital as soon as possible, and even upon seeing Leonard and Rebecca it was tough to comprehend this was really happening. Sorrow filled my heart like never before—a sadness for the loss of our beautiful friend Meagan, and a sadness that my close friends were having to walk this road. We all stood there in that hospital room praying and crying together, but even in those first hours of anguish I was amazed by my friend Leo.

He had a strength and an undeniable reliance and hope in Christ that was visible to us all.

A few days later, as plans were being made for Meagan's service, Leo called me and, to my surprise, said, "I want to lead the first worship song at Meagan's service." I gently asked, "Are you sure?" Leo is an amazing worship leader, but I just could not see how anyone could get up and sing songs of praise, let alone lead other people in worship, during a time like this. His response is one I will never forget, "Sara, I can't tell our congregation each week that they should praise God in the good and bad times if I'm not willing to do it myself." I knew he was right, and I was inspired by his conviction and trust in Jesus. To be honest, though, the producer in me wanted to make sure we had a plan B, just in case he changed his mind.

The evening of Meagan's service, Leo stepped onto the stage and told us the only response he could have during a time like this was to worship God. It was a time of worship like I had never experienced before. As he led the song "Blessed Be Your Name" and sang the lyrics about blessing God's name on the road marked with suffering, I saw a man who had truly put his hope in Christ alone. Leo's trust was centered on God, not his circumstances, and because of that, we were all recipients of the overflow he had through the power of the Holy Spirit. He was able to have God's joy and peace during one of life's most painful circumstances. Still today, that hope continues to overflow into each of us who are fortunate enough to call him and Rebecca our friends, and to those who hear about their journey and Meagan's amazing life.

I want to live with that kind of overflow in my life! I want the prayer that Paul prays in Romans 15:13 to be true of me. This prayer sums it up; as we trust in Christ alone, He will do the rest. My hope is that I trust in God alone, not in the hope of what He can do for me, whether or not I have a job, or even my health or family. In my life and my ministry God is teaching me that in order for Him to fill me with joy and peace, I need to be emptied of myself. Only then can I experience the overflow of God's Spirit—like my friend Leo.

Today's Prayer

Lord, help me fix my eyes on you. May my trust be in you alone and not in the things you can do for me. Empty me of my selfishness and my desire to control the plan you have for me. Fill me with your joy and peace, no matter what road in life you call me to, and let my hope in you overflow by the power of your Spirit. Lord, make us a community of people that overflow into each other's lives because of the hope we have in you!

Sara Emmerson
Creative Arts Producer
Christ Community Church
St. Charles, Illinois

46 ······• RESCUED

> We did not follow cleverly devised stories when we told you about the coming of our Lord Jesus Christ in power, but we were eyewitnesses of his majesty. *(2 Peter 1:16)*

I grew up in the church. My story is like a lot of people's: parents really involved; Mom in the choir; Dad on the board of directors; I attended lock-ins, youth camps, and conventions; got baptized at age twelve, and was mostly a pretty good Christian girl. Then at age thirty-five my world got turned upside down—not from a health crisis, a rocky spot in my marriage, a job loss, or even a wayward child. Nope, my topsy-turvy world happened when I started graduate school. All of a sudden I was out from under the shelter of the safe Christian world I had created, and what I read, saw, and heard awakened questions I had buried deep inside myself. What if the philosophers, researchers, and sociologists I was reading about were right? What if you did get to construct your own truth? What if we were the ones determining what is real and what isn't? What if Jesus is just a nice guy who is good at memorizing the Jewish scriptures? What if all the stories I had been told as a child, read as a young adult, and staked my life on as a pastor's wife are just stories? *What if?* This season began a journey toward truth that I wouldn't trade for anything. I had the amazing opportunity to write down everything I thought and believed to be true about God, the world, and me on dozens of 3" x 5" cards. With this "theology" spread out on our dining room table, I began the process of discovering who God is.

Truth is, the biblical stories about kings dancing, adulterous women being forgiven, water being turned into wine, lame people walking, and doubters believing were never just stories. They were the foundational cement that would support the restoration of humanity. They are what is true about God. So now, all these years later, I work in a church. And when I'm with this community of people I love, I'm once again aware that those of us who have seen God working and been witness to the miraculousness of Him have got to write, sing, design, speak, dance, paint, create, and celebrate THE story—the story that reminds us He would do it all over again if only for our rescue.

Today's Prayer

God, I'm so grateful for your story and the way it writes itself in my heart over and over again. What a miracle your love for me is—that your majesty and power are mine, but not just mine alone. Help me to be aware, to see you at work in the world, and then to somehow, somewhere, some way tell the story. Amen.

Suze Fair
Director of Expression and Communication
Fellowship Missionary Church
Fort Wayne, Indiana

47 ·········• THE DESERT PATH

Trust in the Lord with all your heart and lean not on your own understanding; in all your ways acknowledge him, and he will make your paths straight. *(Proverbs 3:5-6)*

Years ago I had an opportunity to go to the desert to seek guidance from God.

It wasn't exactly the Egyptian wilderness of the desert fathers of ancient days. It was, well, a California state park, complete with groomed trails, guides, and tourists in Hawaiian shirts and sandals. But ever since my wife, Corinne, and I had arrived in the Golden State for a much-needed vacation, I had the uncanny sense that I was *supposed* to take a side trip into the desert. I wondered if God might speak to me in some way—a sort of "burning bush" that might guide my choices at a very confusing crossroads.

I arrived in the park and walked the path, taking in rock formations, the sky, the desert vibe, letting my thoughts percolate. After a while the trail led up a hill, and toward the top I could make out a shape like a cross. *This is it,* I thought. I hiked up the rest of the way full of expectation, senses heightened. Something significant was here.

I clambered up the hill, anticipation growing with every step. I reached the crest, and the vista of the desert land opened up gloriously before me. I approached what turned out to be a cross-shaped sign, and the message came into view:

PLEASE STAY ON TRAIL.

I laughed at myself and my overblown expectations. It had been posted by the park service for the safety of the tourists!

But then I thought further: *Maybe there's a message for me here anyway.*

I had followed one career path, one chosen ministry, for decades. Recently the terrain had changed significantly, leaving me uncertain how to proceed. For months I had been mulling over the unsettling idea of diverting from the path I had followed for so long. Compounding the angst of the moment, Corinne was now wrestling with some serious health issues. So here at the top of the hill, my encounter with this wooden sign seemed like more than a coincidence. I decided to follow the metaphor with my feet. I stayed on the trail. I hiked back down and continued further on. The path narrowed, becoming rockier and increasingly dry and desolate, like the surface of the moon. Nothing could grow here. Off in the distance, the trail wound up another hill, far steeper, positively treacherous. I stopped and looked carefully at the scene. Somewhere inside I sensed God's voice saying, "No matter how narrow and desolate your path toward the future may seem now, no matter how rocky and fraught with dangers, please stay on the trail."

And I listened. My spirit resonated.

Several years later, by God's grace, I'm still on the path, staying the course He has carved out for me as He continues, step by step, to provide in surprising, unforeseen ways. My flimsy faith is slowly growing into something that just might survive even when the trail is narrowest and the terrain most rocky.

And—as far as I can see and imagine—as Robert Frost might say, "that has made all the difference."

Today's Prayer

Good Shepherd, Perfect Guide, as we travel on, help us see your navigating hand, your guidance and provision, the perfection of your vision. We submit our every hope to you. Align us with your Spirit, and hear our longing as we ask, O Lord, for wisdom. Amen.

Greg Ferguson
Writer, Idea Guy, Worship Leader, Experience Designer
Willow Creek Association
South Barrington, Illinois

48 ······• MY UNFINISHED LIFE

Being confident of this, that he who began a good work in you will
carry it on to completion until the day of Christ Jesus.
(Philippians 1:6)

A couple of years ago, I came to the realization that I live in this constant place of unfinished space. Almost everywhere I look in the world around me, I see an unfinished life. My unfinished life. Oh, it's not that things never get completed. I will complete a meal, a phone conversation or coffee with a friend, a workout at the gym. I complete scripts and books and an occasional painting—even this devotional you're now reading. I complete many things, but there is still so much more to be finished. So much left unfinished. And in all that *unfinishedness*—if we can even call it a word—are empty spaces longing to be filled.

I see it in my heart. I see it in my life.

Do you?

I had a few minutes today to just stop and sit on a bench near the mission in San Juan Capistrano. Before me was a series of three red brick arches, one right after another, filled with nothing but empty space. That makes them arches, doesn't it? Through the arches, I focused on the shop windows displaying their wares, green plants here and there, and antique white walls contrasted by deep blue skies. The arches were empty, but that empty space contained beautiful colors and shapes and dimensions that, had that space been filled, my eyes wouldn't have seen.

For every creative person, artist, dreamer, and follower of Christ, we have to remember the importance of that empty space. We must not neglect that unfinished place where the Holy Spirit gently reminds me my life is not designed to be finished. Any sense of completeness I'm designed to have or experience is the meaning and fulfillment found in Christ alone. Purpose, relationship, and satisfaction in this life? Certainly yes! But not a finished life.

The reality that my life is unfinished is the very thing that keeps me moving forward. The empty space is the place to rest in God's grace, trusting He is completing what He started. He has promised to finish not just a few things in our lives, but everything. The Master will not leave His works undone.

It is in these empty spaces, in the very arches of our lives, that I pray God will show us exactly the things He wants us to see: *the colors of grace seen through empty space.*

Today's Prayer

> *Lord, forgive me when my desire is to see finished what you, in your mysterious wisdom, are still working on. Help me to look through the arch of my life to see what you want me to see. I pray for the grace to trust you in all the unfinished places and spaces in my life that you see and know so well. Amen.*

Joey O'Connor
The Grove Center for the Arts & Media
San Clemente, California

49 ·······• MYSTIC PIZZA

It's who you are and the way you live that count before God.
(John 4:23 TM)

One afternoon when our daughter was four years old, she and I were out on the sidewalk when a pizza deliveryman drove up across the street. As he got out of his car, steaming hot pizza in hand, I said to her, "Oooh, Honey, let's make that man give us that pizza!" Looking up from her tricycle with wide brown eyes she asked in her squeaky little-girl voice, "But, why, Daddy? That's not *your* pizza!"

Her innocent question has never left me. Why would I want what isn't mine? Isn't that the root of sin itself? To desire something not rightfully our own, even as Satan desired to be worshiped as God? With one question she uncovered in me the abysmal breach of original sin, that endless chasm of man's separation from God and his futile pursuit of filling a void only God can fill. I had no good answer why I would want the neighbor's pizza.

Aside from realizing that I was being a poor example to my child that day, I began to see more clearly that I often engaged in the sin of comparing myself with others. I not only coveted other people's possessions regularly but also judged myself as always being somehow *less than* others. And, even worse, I saw that I had begun to subtly accuse God of not being just—of actually being unfair to me—for making me who I am, as if He had made some cosmic mistake by creating me as He did.

Pride can move in two directions; arrogance isn't necessarily the opposite of low self-esteem. What I began to learn from my daughter's childlike question is that God always looks at our hearts. He is worshiped more fully when I accept His sovereignty and trust He has given me what He desires me to have—from the way my nose is shaped to the kind of car I drive. Psalm 139 says it was He who formed me in my mother's womb. Who am I to question Him in His sovereign artistry?

Covetousness in any form is my desire to make more of myself, to own or possess something I think will fill an empty space in me that is only shaped for God. Nowadays, whenever I see a pizza deliveryman, I smile and remember that little redhead on her tricycle looking up at me, with freckled cheeks and bright eyes, and I hear the voice of God again.

Today's Prayer

Gracious Father, thank you for the voices of children who speak truth to us in so many ways. Give us ears to hear you in their words. Remind us you are Lord of all, sovereign in every way, and you are eternally just. Amen.

John Chisum
Pastor of Celebration Arts
Fair Haven Ministries
Grand Rapids, Michigan

50 ········• VOICE RECOGNITION

My sheep listen to my voice; I know them, and they follow me.
(John 10:27)

Have you ever misheard or misunderstood someone? How about in your relationship with God?

We have all been given an incredible gift—the divine ability to actually hear God. Amazing! It's clear from Scripture that anything we know of God, He himself has revealed. Our job is to learn our Father's voice—the Shepherd's voice—and to *know* it.

My son, Jackson, knows my voice. In fact, a few minutes after he was born, as he began to cry, I picked him up and sang a song I'd sung many times in the previous nine months. He immediately stopped crying, because he recognized my voice. Remarkably, we have been given that same ability. However, now almost seven years later, I am having to teach my son how to *really* hear and listen to me. The chaos of life, friends, and video games has made it so that my words of instruction, affection, and information sometimes fall on deaf ears. Distracted ears. So we have a little mantra in the Ramsay house that Jackson knows quite well. All I need to say is, "Jackson, you need to . . ." and I hold three fingers in the air. He then says, "Listen, understand, and respond."

It's the same way in our relationship with God. The ability to hear Him is a gift, but we have a tremendous role and responsibility in that communicating relationship. We must learn to listen, understand, and respond. Here are a few practical things you can do to move in that direction today.

First, know God is speaking to you already. You need to put yourself in the posture of listening. Start by eliminating noise from your life. Pray. Ponder. Sit quietly. *Listen.* This is not the lifestyle or pace that our culture defaults to. Understand that you may be addicted to the fast-paced, multitasking, TV-invading, Facebook-ing, microwave-is-too-slow lifestyle. If you are like me, you need to find another gear that slows you down from the fast-paced freeway of normal life. Learn the art of quiet. Find it. Fight for it. Wake up early for it if you have to.

Next, you need to understand what God is saying. Here is where you need to include some other people in your journey. Self-actualization of your own story is one of the most difficult things you as a human can do. It is much easier for some wise counsel—emphasis on wise, not just available counsel—to speak into your life and see the story God is writing. Then take this information and pray, ponder, and reflect.

Finally, *move*, and move quickly. God is moving. His kingdom is on the move. Don't miss out on the piece He has specifically designed for you to be a part of. Respond. If you only do steps one and two, it's like the millions of unwritten songs that plague our world. Don't be an unwritten song. Play the chord. Write the lyric. Finish well, because at the end of every rainbow is a large pot of doughnuts. Try the jelly!

Today's Prayer

Lord, help me eliminate the noise and distractions of life and listen as you comfort and lead me. May I never miss out on your plans for me. Amen.

Jon Ramsay
Worship Pastor
Mariners Church
Mission Viejo, California

51 ·········• THE BEAUTY OF BROKEN PIECES

"For I know the plans I have for you," declares the LORD, "plans to prosper you and not to harm you, plans to give you hope and a future. Then you will call on me and come and pray to me, and I will listen to you. You will seek me and find me when you seek me with all your heart. I will be found by you," declares the LORD, "and will bring you back from captivity. I will gather you from all the nations and places where I have banished you," declares the LORD, "and will bring you back to the place from which I carried you into exile."
(Jeremiah 29:11-14)

As an artist, it's easy for me to look at a completed piece of art and marvel at the uniqueness and beauty of the work while often missing the detail that went into it. It's true of my life, too. I often look at my successes and accomplishments as the moments that define me. But what about the events and moments that leave me feeling helpless and alone?

Not long ago I encountered a season of life unlike any other I had experienced before. It seemed like everything I knew about myself and life was being challenged, and I found myself unsure of all the things I typically would have put my confidence in. I was right smack in the middle of a desert experience, and I was scared, confused, and tired. My life seemed to lack any glimmer of hope.

I remember seeing a kaleidoscope one night, and I thought about all the broken pieces of glass contained in that kaleidoscope. On their own they were just useless pieces of glass that you and I would most likely throw away. Looking through that long cylinder, though, I saw something different. As the light reflected off the pieces of glass, a beautiful pattern of color and symmetry began to appear. With each turn of the cylinder a new pattern appeared and was even more amazing than the one before.

As I thought about my life that night, I was reminded that it's not just my accomplishments and successes God uses. He uses the brokenness, too. Just like the kaleidoscope, God desires to shine His light through me to create beauty. As a worship leader, I now know God desires to use not only my skills and abilities but my brokenness as well. In fact, that's what allows Him to shine the most.

Today's Prayer

God, thank you that I can go into this day confidently knowing you are everything I need. You desire to give my life hope and a future if I will only surrender it to you. Thank you for shining your light through the broken pieces of my life and creating true beauty that allows others to see you even more. Amen.

Scott Leggett
Pastor of Worship Arts
Grace Chapel
Englewood, Colorado

52 ....• EXCELLENT LEADING

> He chose David his servant and took him from the sheep pens; from
> tending the sheep he brought him to be the shepherd of his people
> Jacob, of Israel his inheritance. And David shepherded them with
> integrity of heart; with skillful hands he led them. *(Psalm 78:70-72)*

I am new to the full-time position of worship leader. I've been watching and learning from many wonderful, qualified worship leaders for more than thirty years, though. Little by little, God has been entrusting me with opportunities to lead His people and preparing me for where I am today. I am now entering my fifth year in this important and humbling role. What a privilege!

It occurs to me, as I study the life of one of the preeminent worship leaders in Scripture, that there is much to learn from David's example. In this passage, we see God called David from humble beginnings to do great things for His glory. That's a good reminder to us—that God can use any willing and humble servant, regardless of his or her background or station in life. I'm not denying the role that *skill* plays, but we'll get to that later.

There are four aspects of the job of worship leader that are mentioned in these verses. First, it says David became the *shepherd* of God's people. This same word is often used in place of the word *pastor.* It reminds me that I must have a pastor's heart while leading my worship team, my choir, and my congregation. My first call, of course, is to honor and bless God, but it's also important for me to care for and edify the people God has given me to lead.

Second, it says David led the people with *integrity of heart.* I must be real with people. It's easy to fall into pride or pretense when leading, but our worshipers love and follow leaders they can trust. I must resist putting a worship set together that manipulates people into a false, emotional sense of worship. I need to lead them to know and see Jesus and be overwhelmed by Him alone.

The third quality of David's leading is that he *guided* them. This is the leader part of the term *worship leader.* We often only focus on the worship part, forgetting that God has called us to encourage our people and instruct them in what true worship is. As worship "shepherds," we can feel free to weave Scripture throughout our worship leading that reinforces or explains what we're singing.

Finally, David led them with *skillful* hands. If God's name is majestic (Psalm 8:1), and we are encouraged to set our minds on things that are excellent (Philippians 4:8), then our worship leading in His name must be done excellently. How many times, maybe in a busy week, have I been tempted to just throw something together and depend on my own natural ability to make it look good? He gave me the ability in the first place! Who He is compels us to always offer up our very best to Him.

Today's Prayer

Father, may both our worship and our leading be pleasing to you, our excellent Lord. Amen.

Steve Lively
Pastor of Worship and Care
The Bridge Bible Fellowship
Reseda, California

ABOUT STAN ENDICOTT

STAN ENDICOTT is a nationally recognized, deeply respected and beloved worship pastor, music producer, and mentor to hundreds of worship leaders. He serves on part-time staff at Mariners Church in Irvine, CA as worship leader. He has produced hundreds of albums for Maranatha Music and produced gospel choirs for many internationally-known ministries including Franklin Graham, Greg Laurie, Promise Keepers, and Youth With A Mission (YWAM). He is a consultant with the Willow Creek Church in Chicago and Saddleback Church in Lake Forest, California.

Stan has a bachelor's degree in music composition and is founder and partner of the Slingshot Group. Slingshot serves churches in strategy and staffing, focusing on worship leaders and tech arts <slingshotgroup .net>. Stan's heart is for mentoring, "aiming," and training young worship leaders and artists. Stan has a rare combination of expertise, experience, and avant-garde thinking. His ahead-of-the-curve methodology led him to step out in faith and provide churches and communities of all sizes with relevant music and help them unleash the power of music in their congregations.

Stan and his wife, Connie, have been married for thirty-seven years. They have three children and four grandchildren. They live in Irvine, California.

Quiet Moments for Worship Leaders is a collection of daily meditations and devotionals that invite worship leaders, pastors, and other members to step away from the noise and stress of their day and spend a few moments in quietness with God. Using the ageless writings of the Book of Psalms, Marty Parks explores how the writers' passion for worship, their love of God's word, and even their colossal failures, offer us comfort and inspire us to infuse our lives with the strength and truth of His Word.

Quiet Moments for Worship Leaders
Scriptures, Meditations, and Prayers
Marty Parks
ISBN: 978-0-8341-2372-4

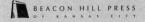 BEACON HILL PRESS
OF KANSAS CITY

www.beaconhillbooks.com
facebook.com/beaconhillpress
Available online or wherever books are sold.

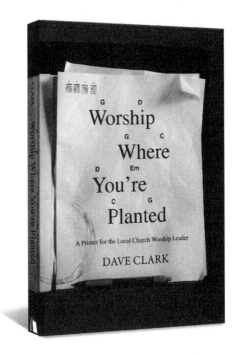

Worship Where You're Planted seeks to recognize and respond to the situations that worship leaders encounter. Through exploration and insight, author Dave Clark tackles issues such as transitioning between worship leaders, navigating between traditional and contemporary music styles, and building rapport with the congregation. With wisdom and understanding, Clark helps small and midsize churches find comfort and connection as they lead their congregations in worship.

Worship Where You're Planted
A Primer for the Local Church Worship Leader
Dave Clark
ISBN: 978-0-8341-2555-1

BEACON HILL PRESS
OF KANSAS CITY

www.beaconhillbooks.com
facebook.com/beaconhillpress
Available online or wherever books are sold.